The
Reluctant
Weekend Gardener

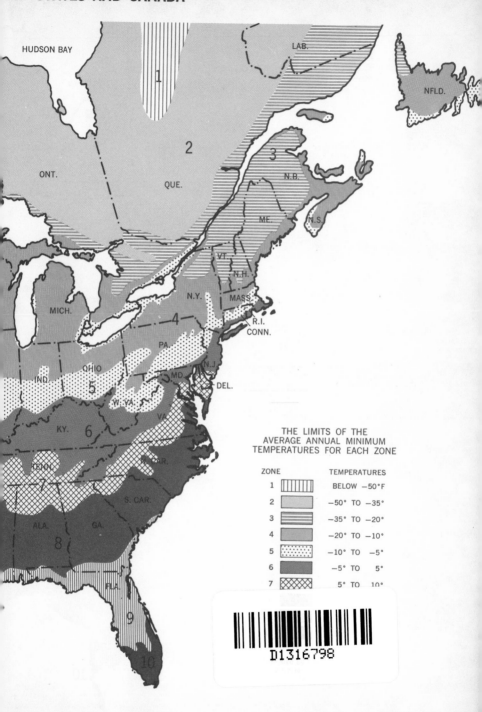

THE LIMITS OF THE
AVERAGE ANNUAL MINIMUM
TEMPERATURES FOR EACH ZONE

ZONE		TEMPERATURES
1		BELOW −50°F
2		−50° TO −35°
3		−35° TO −20°
4		−20° TO −10°
5		−10° TO −5°
6		−5° TO 5°
7		5° TO 10°

D1316798

The Reluctant Weekend Gardener

CARLA WALLACH

Illustrations by Alfred Anthony, Jr.

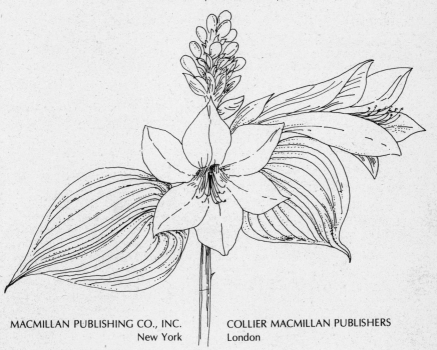

MACMILLAN PUBLISHING CO., INC.
New York

COLLIER MACMILLAN PUBLISHERS
London

To Marie Killilea,
who lovingly pushed and nagged me
into this book,
and to my husband, Philip,
who was more or less patient
throughout the labor pains

Library of Congress Cataloging in Publication Data

Wallach, Carla.
　　The reluctant weekend gardener.

　　Bibliography: p.
　　1. Gardening. I. Title.
SB453.W23　　　　　　　　635.9　　　　　　　73-15701
ISBN 0-02-623150-6

Macmillan Publishing Co., Inc.
866 Third Avenue, New York, N.Y. 10022
Collier-Macmillan Canada Ltd.

Library of Congress Catalog Number: 73-15701

First Printing 1973

Printed in the United States of America

Contents

Acknowledgments

I have drawn extensive information from many books and periodicals too numerous to list here, but these sources will be found in the Bibliography. Special thanks are due, for her help in checking my notes and offering valuable suggestions, to Miss Elizabeth C. Hall, Senior Librarian, The Horticultural Society of New York and Associate Curator of Education Emeritus, The New York Botanical Garden.

For several years, my "home away from home" has been The New York Botanical Garden where their many courses have been a source of delight as well as knowledge. To their instructors I owe much. I can't overlook the many pleasant hours spent at the Brooklyn Botanic Garden or the youngest "baby" I watched develop into the vibrant community center it now is, the Queens Botanical Garden. The fact that it chose to establish itself next door to where I play tennis helped to cut down considerably on my research time! Special permission to visit their greenhouses is deeply appreciated.

Introduction

There is nothing more exasperating to a beginner than to pick up a book by an expert who proceeds to tell him how easy it all is—whatever "it" is. This can be tennis, golf, knitting, cooking in the Arctic—or even gardening.

I know. When my husband and I bought a weekend house in the country a few years ago (in itself a story of folly unlimited), I barely knew the difference between a geranium and a petunia, and my husband didn't even know that. To make matters worse, the house came with a large empty greenhouse. I immediately bought every book available on every phase of gardening, and joined countless flower and plant "clubs." This only added confusion and despair to my ignorance. It remained for experience—that tired cliché—to teach me. Not that I am a genuine expert now—I want to make that as clear, firm and loud as possible.

This book is not for the experienced gardener. It's not for the hobbyist gardener. Quite frankly, it's not even for those who like gardening and have a lot of time to do it. Who is it for, then? A lot of people. The millions of part-time gardeners with second homes to whom every minute of a weekend is precious; business couples living in the suburbs, tired at the end of a working week, ready for some fun and relaxation with friends; anyone, young or old, retired or active, who just has other things on his mind besides gardening when it comes to leisure time. It's recreation versus horticulture.

1

What all of us want in our "club" of part-time gardeners is a no-nonsense guide that tells it like it is—all the nitty-gritty pitfalls to avoid, skipping in-depth reasons for composting or building a dry well. Dr. Livingstone's famous quote applies to just about everything in life, including gardening: "It wasn't the lions and tigers that got us—it was the gnats." Once a person becomes a genuine expert in any field, it's so easy for him to forget those "gnats." He's come a long way since those early days of "hit or miss" experiences. Well, I haven't. I'm still there and learning. I've discovered, the hard way, how to read between the lines. Seemingly innocent paragraphs describing the virtues of a plant will disclose, upon a hard second look, that to maintain these said virtues demands hours of your time. To some, this is well worthwhile. To you and to me—forget it.

Yet, let's face reality. We've made an investment in a piece of property and we want the value to go up, not down. Also, the mere fact that we don't want to work too hard at it doesn't mean that we don't want and can't appreciate a beautiful garden in attractive grounds. If it sounds like we want to have our cake and eat it too, you're right. Why not be honest about it? The cake may not end up winning a gold medal, but let me assure you that it'll taste mighty good! It *can* be done; this I know from personal experience.

A final word—on words. Each field has its own special "language." "Gardenese" is no better than a doctor's prescription. Try to understand what it says, in Latin or English. I want to assure you right now that subtitles will not be needed for this book. Too many of my gardening friends complain about this, and I made a mental note of it. (Not that I could do it anyway, I must confess!) During the whole time I wrote this book, I kept foremost in mind one picture: that of a normal, intelligent person who knows absolutely nothing about gardening—and, what's more, has no ambition of becoming President of the local Garden Club. Maybe the Golf Club? Well, that's another story!

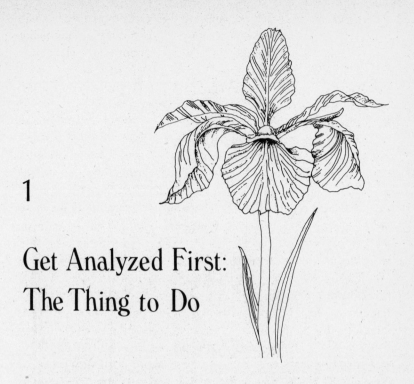

1

Get Analyzed First:
The Thing to Do

Lie back, relax; I promise this will be painless. Just a few questions and comments about your lifestyle so we can write the right prescription for you. We've already established your hang-up. You've bought the most beautiful new boat in the world, and your weekend house is just a place to dry out between sails. Or you and your wife commute all week long to your jobs in the city, and comes Saturday your stamina is below sea level. Or maybe you've just got a chronic bad back (join the millions of others) and bending over more than six times a day sends you into a spasm.

You all share the same no-no: gardening is somewhere at the bottom of the list of things you'd most like to do on any given weekend. But, alas, like your mortgage, it won't go away by your just brooding about it. You could sell the house or leave your wife (everybody knows the wife always gets to keep the house), but we'll save these drastic solutions for last. In the meantime, get ready. And be honest now, because the type of garden and overall landscaping that will be the most suitable for you, in terms of getting the best results for the least amount of time and effort spent, will depend to a large degree on your answers.

First, who does the gardening in your family—husband or wife, or both? What is the maximum time each weekend that you want to devote to gardening? (Don't be ashamed to say only one hour. There's always asphalt and a can of green paint, you know.) Are you under thirty, middle-aged or retired? This is not a frivolous question. Muscle power plays a far greater role in gardening than the experts ever let on. I know you can be a weakling at only twenty-eight, and a Tarzan at sixty, but don't hedge the issue. Lifting heavy bags of fertilizer or mulch, digging and preparing a new flower bed, and handling many power tools all demand a strong back and a healthy constitution. For those lacking such strength, there are still many ways of obtaining a lovely garden. Knowing your drawbacks beforehand will help solve your problems.

A little about money, now. Can you afford outside help? If so, how often and for how long? And if you can afford it, is there a source of part-time gardeners in your area? Do you know the hourly rate? Answering that last one should give you a bit more motivation to go out there and rake a few leaves. Obviously, the size and scope of your garden (when I say "garden," I mean the entire grounds surrounding the house) depend on the amount of time and work that will be devoted to it. This is why these questions are so important. If husband and wife and a part-time gardener all put in half a day every weekend to outdoor work, you will naturally have results different from those of a golf widow who can only work a few hours all by herself.

A word should be said at this point about children: no. Don't depend on them. No longer can the head of the family bring his authority to bear on making his teen-agers labor in his fields. The

4

same is true of neighbors' children. In this affluent society they work only when in sudden need of money, like a week before Mother's Day or Christmas. You're in luck when they've finally received permission to buy a motorcycle or a car or a boat—they usually have to pay for it themselves, and then comes all that maintenance! But these are occasional bursts of labor, and a garden unfortunately doesn't grow that way. It's wiser not to count on this source for extra help. Look upon it as a bonus when it does happen.

What about your own children? Do you have any, and if so, what are their ages? They may be at the stage when fishing trips, camping, baseball games are all a precious part of childhood, and you want to be a part of it while it lasts. Later on, as children become teen-agers, parents have more time on their hands—if not on the telephone. If your children are pre-school age, forget about poor mother being the gardener. Do you travel a great deal during the summer months? Are you an athletic nut? (Don't be shy, I'm one.) You're sitting pretty if it's tennis or swimming. A few hours at the most and you've had it. But if you're a golfer or a sailor, that's a full day affair and spells trouble for your garden—if you're the gardener in the family. If the wife does it all, the husband is off the hook. Of course, if both of you enjoy sports, then be prepared for pachysandra carpeting, fence-to-fence.

We've covered "Who you are" and "How you live"—now let's get on to "Where you are." The location of your gardening site is vital. Take weekend gardeners with seashore or lake-front homes: they get a real break because usually the property is small and the natural terrain prohibits any large-scale gardening. The beach cottage has its picturesque sand dunes, and the lake cabin is surrounded by majestic pines. Not much is needed to make these two types of homesites attractive. The suburban house, on the other hand, is much more formal, sometimes with a (shudder!) manicured look. The weekend house in deep country seems to be made to order for masses of flowers, herbs, vegetables, fruits, shrubs. That's if you lack will power.

By now, if you've answered all the questions truthfully, a definite pattern should have emerged indicating your limitations. Once you have faced up to the fact that so many or few hours a week is *it* that you and/or your wife and/or outside help can spare, you are on the road to successful weekend gardening. You can plan your garden realistically, with no regrets or guilt feelings. In fact, you may actually find yourself enjoying your garden (which is really what it's all about), precisely because you won't have knocked yourself out caring for it.

I was tempted to illustrate how this self-analysis can be applied to imaginary couples, but I feel you'll agree with me that no two situations are ever the same. You merely end by generalizing so broadly that no reader can relate to it. What's important is that *you* have a mental picture of *your* needs. The following chapter shows you, step by step, how to translate these needs into reality. Keep these modest at the start. It's easier to add later on than it is to cut down from, say, five flower beds to three. Is that ever a mess! I was faced with doing just that. Don't ask, just take my word for it.

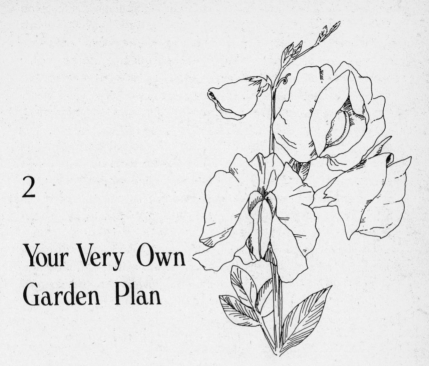

2

Your Very Own Garden Plan

The moment of truth has arrived. Now that you and your family have been thoroughly analyzed, and you've taken a cold, long, hard look at your grounds, you know what you want and also what you can't have. Best of all, you're at peace with yourself because you don't have to apologize anymore for putting golf ahead of gardening. You are ready for the "master plan"!

Your tools are simple: a few sheets of graph paper, pencils, eraser, and one of those ruled yellow pads. Depending on the size of your property, let each square on the graph paper equal one square foot. Graph paper comes in different size squares; the larger your property, the smaller the "square" you buy. For ten feet, I simply count ten squares, or on plain paper let one inch equal twenty feet. In any case, don't worry too much about having the plan to the exact, perfect scale. Just don't make the driveway three times wider than the house. Measure your average stride when you're walking, and use that as a fairly good yardstick. On graph paper, outline your property boundaries. Indicate north, south, east and west (as a clue, the sun rises in the east and sets in the west). Put in the house, driveway, entrance, public road.

You will now see that there are three general areas on your property to consider. The first is the one that all the neighbors and strangers see as they drive or walk (if anybody still does that) past your house. If the house is close to the road, they'll see plenty; if it's set back, they'll have to slow down and twist their necks a bit. The entrance, the driveway and the garage are usually in plain sight.

Next comes your own area, where you relax, entertain, play, do anything you want. It's your own private world. The third, the service area, is the one you don't want *anybody* to see, yourself or the neighbors. Things like garbage cans, storage sheds, compost pile (if you go in for that sort of thing), dead branches, etc. are here. If you have small children, somewhere between the service area and the private one you may want to add swings, sandbox, tent or whatever. Their play area should be nearby so you can keep an eye on them, yet you don't want it smack in front of the terrace.

Right here I must confess to something that is antisocial and anti-American: a passion for privacy. I have a totally European outlook on this subject. I just can't understand why so many homes are landscaped elaborately down to the last inch facing the road, and shamefully neglected in the back where all the living takes place! And both front and back are usually exposed to neighbors. It is important to frame the house attractively with plants suitable in type and size to the style of the house, keeping scale and balance in mind. But once that is done, the private world of the owners should get the lion's share of attention. So much for my hang-up!

8

The next thing to do is to outline on your graph paper all the existing trees (obviously major ones only if yours is a heavily wooded area), and shrubs—both around the house (called foundation plants) and those elsewhere on the grounds. Now, on paper, is the time to take out anything you don't want. Sometimes a little "thinning out" is all that's needed. Taking out an overgrown shrub here and there can open up an area and pleasantly change the whole effect.

Foundation plantings are the chief culprits. If unwisely chosen when the house was built, today they can look as though they are strangling the house, preventing air and sun from reaching inside. Or maybe there are too many kinds of plants, one of everything all around the house! Before removing any shrub, give some thought to where else it might be needed. Transplanting is hard work if you do it yourself, and costly if you have it done professionally, so it's a good idea to see if it's worth the effort in the first place. If not, give it away to someone who'll be happy to have it.

Whatever you do, when replacing a shrub, try to choose one that will not need pruning. Know the height at maturity of the plant, and select accordingly. It's enough that you may have to prune back the previous owner's mistakes each year, without adding your own!

You should now have on your graph the house, public road, driveway, entrance, garage, foundation planting, trees and shrubs, service area and your own private area. Add any other prominent items on your property, such as large boulders, rock outcropping, pond, swimming pool or any special sports area, and lawns. Also add any existing flower beds, vegetable gardens, orchards. Now check the need for privacy. When sipping your cocktail on the terrace, can anyone see you, from any side? Do "skinny dipping" in your pool or taking a sunbath naked make you a nervous wreck, thinking a thousand eyes are beaded on you? If yes, then take a second mortgage, do anything, but have an evergreen hedge planted as soon as possible. Evergreens are best because at least you get twelve months' service out of them! Hollies, hemlocks

9

and white pines are fabulous, if they do well in your part of the country. The service area can be screened off by similar use of lower-growing evergreens.

Remember that trees and shrubs form the backbone of your land-scaping, with lawn and/or ground covers the unifying factor. Trees and shrubs that flower are obviously the more desirable choice, for then you get the best of both worlds! These plants stay with you for a long, long time, so do think twice before cutting down or buying any. They give you shade, privacy, shelter from wind, and the lush, green look that sent city dwellers to the country in the first place. Also, and so important—they are virtually care free. Unless some awful blight comes along (as with the gypsy moth or elm disease), trees and shrubs do not require the constant care that fruits, vegetables and flowers do. When fertilizing the lawn each year, you can scatter a few handfuls of the stuff around trees and shrubs that usually border the lawn. If you plant new ones, or transplant any, you must be sure to water them deeply once a week, at least, during the first summer and fall. They need to go into winter with as much moisture in their root systems as possible. As for the established trees and shrubs, just sit back and admire them. (see "Pruning," however, before you get too smug!) Note the list of trees and shrubs at the end of Chapter 3, should you have to go out and buy any.

Now that you have pretty much everything on your graph, see how much you can take *out*. Jot down that list on the yellow pad. We've already commented on trees and shrubs—go easy on these. But what about the lawn? Is most of your property taken up by it? Do you have grass growing on a slope, slight to the eye but not to your muscles when you mow it—or under some trees where it's not doing too well—or in areas and pathways that get so much wear and tear that you see more soil than grass? Consider a ground cover in these situations. In fact, keep thinking ground cover as you survey your property, because once it's planted and established (two years normally, three at the very most, depending on how closely you place the plants), your work is ended!

At first glance, it would seem that grass is still the least expensive type of groundcover when compared with the initial cost of putting in standard ground cover plants. But it would be most revealing to keep a record of how much the fertilizers cost year after year, plus all the anti-this and anti-that (also every year) to cope with all those weeds and diseases, plus the seed itself, plus the costly power tools. If you have a large area, a ridermower is a must—and that's not cheap! I'm not even taking into account the labor of doing all the above, as well as raking leaves and mowing. Now, I'm not against a lawn; almost all homes need some of it. I'm merely suggesting that you consider cutting down its size in order to reduce the work. Nothing, but nothing, is more irritating, time-consuming and back-breaking than "edging" or "trimming" a lawn. This means cutting the grass anywhere the mower can't reach, and it's usually done by hand—with hedge clippers or with a power tool that is maddening because of the narrow area it covers or because its battery has just run out. Wise old gardeners on large estates used to say "three hours of trimming for every hour of mowing."

Here is where you must use your imagination and all the tricks available to avoid this tiresome "trimming" chore. If yours is a small area and the garden design is on the formal side, as might be found in the suburbs, you may consider curved, paved mowing strips, on the same level as the grass, so that the mower can go over lawn and strip at the same time, cutting the grass right to the very edge. The curving design prevents having to make an awkward back and forth motion with the mower when you get to corners. Concrete, bricks or wood can be used to make the strip. Gravel or crushed stone is tricky because it can spill over and get in the mower—and goodbye blades—and wood chips can be scattered during a strong wind storm. The strip can be used anywhere the lawn wanders: next to flower beds, steps, walls, trees. To look its best, the strip installation is really a job for the professional and can be expensive, which is why I emphasized the relative smallness of the area to be done.

11

For larger and less formal areas, I much prefer a "natural" strip of ground cover. To me it is far more attractive and "at home" in such a setting. Ground covers are tough and rapid growers, so if you clip some off accidentally with the mower it's no great tragedy. (See the chapter on ground covers for a list of suitable ones.) Certainly, under shrubs and around foundation plantings, ground covers are a must. An attractive mulch is very good and can be used, but a natural "carpet of green" has the edge every time, in my opinion.

To continue with what you can take *out* of your existing garden, look for flower beds that are seldom seen. I'm the first to admit (because I did it myself) that it's delightful at the end of the day to take drink in hand and stroll through your grounds into the woods or a lower field, or perhaps turn a corner in a remote part of your garden and come up, quite suddenly, to a lovely drift of flowers that you lovingly planted there. They might be tender bulbs, annuals, house plants taken out and placed there for the summer, or perennials. But because they are in a semi- or entirely-wild part of your property, weeds will have a field day taking over. Heavy mulching would help, but it looks out of place in a naturalistic setting. And watering is a nightmare if a severe dry spell forces you to carry pails of water back and forth. Ask yourself if seeing this flower bed once a day at the most is worth the effort.

Only those beds which are in full view of the terrace, and which also can be seen and admired from inside the house, are worth the time and work. If your outdoor life centers around the swimming pool, concentrate on landscaping that area. If you spend most of your time on the terrace, then obviously that's the spot to dramatize. (Remember those questions on "Who Are You"? Well, this is where you translate the answers into action.) If you're in an area where the bugs zoom in straight for your veins from four o'clock on, day in, day out, and you therefore spend most of your leisure time inside a screened-in porch, then hanging baskets and tubs of plants are for you, transforming this second living room into an outdoor garden.

12

What else can you take out or change? Anything that has to be clipped into a neat design. Frankly, it's not even attractive, outside of Versailles and such places. A typical small suburban plot with hedges and shrubs clipped into mounds, pyramids, cones and what not is absurdly pretentious. It's a Scarsdale Walter Mitty dream of Hampton Court. There are still some estates left in the United States where a long, curving driveway suddenly opens to reveal a superb mansion set in park-like surroundings. Formally clipped hedges look at ease there, as does any form of topiary. These create natural boundaries between the grounds close to the house, used for entertaining and strolling, and the wild meadows and pastures beyond. But back to reality. You don't have a head gardener and staff under him. You're *it*, remember? So be grateful that leaving hedges and shrubs alone not only will make your home grounds look better, but will mean *no* work for you. That's *if* you select these plants wisely. (See the list on pages 37-42.)

Try to have as many outside water faucets as possible. These outlets allow you to drag a relatively short length of hose around when watering flower beds or newly planted shrubs. At best, a hose is really a pain to uncoil and pull over the grass, catching it in low limbs as you turn corners. You do the watering and then repeat the whole business going back. One of those extra-large green wooden tubs is excellent for storing hose. They're attractive, and you can coil fifty feet of hose in them easily, which is the maximum length you can handle. Several of these scattered around outside the house will save you labor and sore muscles.

Perhaps there's little you can do about your entrance and driveway, short of a major job requiring the skills of a landscape architect and a crew of men. But if it's too narrow (the most common complaint) and bordered by lawn, this is your golden opportunity to kill two birds with one stone. Cut into the lawn (thereby reducing lawn work) and widen the driveway by covering the grass with whatever your driveway is made of. I have yet to see a driveway that is too wide, and I don't mean only when one is having a large party. Consider the number of cars the average family owns

13

today (the more children, the more cars), delivery vans, oil trucks, garbage trucks, etc. The way to judge the ideal width for a driveway is to picture two trucks passing each other. Would one or both have to go over the grass? Or would one have to back up? Naturally, you can't make space where it doesn't exist. But *if* you have it, use it intelligently.

For a driveway to be almost maintenance-free (nothing in life is 100% maintenance-free!), it should be made of some kind of paving rather than gravel or crushed stone. Asphalt, macadam or bricks are there to stay, once permanently put down. The only danger is scraping by the snowplow in winter. Any type of crushed stone is far more "natural" and attractive in a rural country setting, but it exacts its price: monthly raking to keep it smooth and free of debris (and leaves in the fall). Come spring, the snowplow has made a horrid mess of it, scattering stones here and there all over the lawn. You never rake back the exact amount that was displaced, so every two years or so you have to order a few truckloads more.

Of course, if you live in a snow-free part of the country, this problem doesn't exist, and you may wish to indulge yourself in this bit of luxury. (I do, and I cope with snow as well—but then my idiosyncrasy is that I intensely dislike anything that resembles a city street set in the country.) You know the pros and cons, so it's up to you to decide. Another factor might be the length of the driveway. If it's very long, believe me when I say it'll require maintenance as outlined above; if it's a short driveway-entry court type, then the extra bit of effort may well be worth it for the esthetic rewards. Should I add that whatever type you have or choose, the driveway should slope gently *away* from the house and garage? Drainage is important—indeed vital—in those states with heavy rainfall and/or snow.

Go into your garden and look over your whole property with your paper plan in hand. The plan has its value, but remember that nothing replaces the real thing "in the flesh." It's like ordering something by catalog; you have the item down to its last inch in dimensions, color, shape, photograph, etc., but it isn't until it

14

arrives and you unwrap it that you *know* how it really looks and how it will fit. The same goes for your garden plan. Your eye reveals a vista that the paper can't translate, a pussywillow hidden by underbrush, a magnificent boulder behind tall weeds. Train your eye not to be surprised by the unexpected, to search out the unusual. Perhaps you'll find it, perhaps you won't. But you will know your grounds thoroughly by then, and will undertake with confidence whatever changes you plan to make. You will be working *with* nature and not against it. What you may look upon as a disadvantage now may turn out to be the showpiece of your property. It's not what you have as much as what you do with it that counts. You'll make errors; be prepared for them. They'll be minor ones if you've taken the time to draw your plan first on paper as discussed, and if you've inspected your grounds carefully. Before taking off on a plane trip, a knowing traveler always asks himself, as he packs, what can I do without and still look well-dressed and appropriate when I get there? Keep asking yourself the same question about your garden. The more you keep or create, the more work you'll have. There's no simpler way to say it.

As with all the following chapters, an entire book could be written on this one. Landscaping is a skill, an art, acquired after many years of practical experience. There are theories and rules, of course, as taught in many universities and botanical gardens, but it's the *doing* that separates the men from the boys. Those who garden for a hobby don't mind experimenting, changing flower beds around the way a housewife changes furniture in the living room. If yours is a large property with problems, or if you wish to make so many changes that it will involve grading, building retaining walls, elaborate terraces, etc., I would strongly urge you to employ a landscape architect. The American Society of Landscape Architects has chapters in major cities and can be contacted for names and further information. Landscape designers who are frequently affiliated with large nurseries are also a good choice.

If you have ever used an interior designer to re-do your house or apartment, then you'll know how to work with a landscape designer, who does the same sort of thing to your outdoor area. You can pay him a flat consultation fee to tell you what can be done with your grounds, or you can have him purchase the plant material and supervise all the labor for you. His profit, as with interior designers, will be the difference between the wholesale and retail prices. He gets the former, you pay the latter. Detailed plans are obviously extra. However, most weekend homes are not in this elaborate category. Your goal is simplicity of design, and even though this is usually the hardest to achieve (note Japanese gardens or a Norell dress), a massive dose of self-discipline will see you through. Learn to say *no*. Start small. You can always add later, you know.

A major part of landscaping is the selection of plant material. However, you can't know what will do well in your garden unless you have some vague idea of what your soil is all about. A real old hand would sniff it, finger it, roll it in his hands, notice the color, roll his eyeballs heavenward, and tell you precisely what you've got. If you were such a creature you wouldn't be reading this book in the first place, and the odds are none of your friends fit the category. (Some will claim they do, but don't you believe it.) The best way is simply to buy a soil test kit. They come in different types, sizes and prices. You don't need one that will test your soil for every mineral known to man; just buy a nice little kit where you dip the paper in the soil or pour some soil in tiny bottles and, depending on the color it turns, you know whether you have acid, neutral or alkaline soil. I could tell you all about the meaning of pH, but you'd really be bored stiff. Soil with a pH of 6.5 to 7.5 is neutral. Above 7.5 it is alkaline (on the sweet side); below 6.5 it is acid (associate this with wooded areas, leaf-mold).

You could also send soil samples to your Agricultural Experiment Station or Agricultural Extension Service. They will gladly give you an analysis of your soil. But, to be perfectly honest, you won't get around to doing it any more than I did once you are faced with sending for the special container to hold the soil (most states provide this wonderful service free), and then, with a scrupulously clean shovel, taking ten to twenty slivers of the soil, each time washing and drying the shovel, and putting the soil in a clean pail. You sift about a pint of this mixture in the container (or your own *clean* plastic or coffee can) and mail, with detailed notes. It's easier to pick up one of those kits next time you're at the garden center. It's even fun—makes you feel like a mad scientist, crawling from one side of your property to the next, filling little tubes! Tell the kids you're testing for orange moon dust.

Don't panic if you find out that you've got all three types of soil on your property. All it means is that when the house was built, bulldozers played havoc with the soil. Builders are not horticulturists. Sand, cement, rocks, all were discreetly buried under a few inches of their "quick" grass. I run the gamut, from pure, black, undiluted humus to sand, on my grounds. You have one of two choices: select plant material that will be suited to that particular type of soil, or change the soil to suit the plants you want. You'll do better with the first, even if you have to doctor up the soil a bit anyway. Coping with the second may involve a radical change in the pH, and let's face it, every few years you'll have to re-do the test because the soil has a way of reverting back to its original properties (unless you dug a small Grand Canyon and refilled it with fresh soil).

There are chemicals available that will change your soil to your exact specifications: aluminum sulphate or sulphur will increase the acidity of your soil (lower the pH), while ground limestone will make your soil more alkaline (raise the pH). For small areas, this changing of the soil may be worthwhile if you have your heart set on a particular plant, but certainly on any large areas (except lawns when limestone is spread every few years) it is not advisable. Anyway, plants are not really all that fussy, unless yours is a soil of one extreme or the other. With good drainage, and fertilization before planting, you shouldn't have problems. I recall a prominent horticulturist saying that it was a good thing that plants couldn't read—half of them would learn that they shouldn't be growing where they are now! So do test your soil, but don't let it turn you into Madame Curie.

You will next be reading about plants, and checking plant lists. And botanical names. Let me say right now that it's the only "gardenese" that you'll get from me. Unfortunately, there is a good reason for it. The so-called common name of a plant in one part of the country can be quite different in another. The same plant may have several common names, for that matter. The botanical name, on the other hand, is the same the world over. You can order a plant by mail from any nursery anywhere on this globe, and they'll send you precisely what you want if you've used the correct botanical name.

I'll try to make it as painless as possible. A full botanical description of a plant can include the names of the genus, species and variety. Genus describes a family of plants that have broadly similar characteristics (like, let's say, the *Macdougall* clan in Scotland). Species means plants within that family which differ from one another, enough to set them apart (like the Macdougalls of *northern Scotland* versus the Macdougalls of *southern Scotland*). Last, we have the variety, which means a group or class of plants within a species that have slight differences (here it would be like adding *Margaret* Macdougall and her brother *Bruce* of northern Scotland, or *Robert* and his sister *Ann* Macdougall of southern Scotland).

I realize that this is oversimplifying the definition of terms to a dreadful degree, but most authorities admit that it is difficult to define this subject precisely. "Cultivar" has been used in place of or in addition to "variety," but most nurseries don't bother with it. We have to realize that the plant world is fantastically enormous, with infinite variations. It boggles the mind, for instance, when one thinks of orchids: that is one "family" that is broken down into many hundreds of species and varieties. If all you were given was the name Smith or Brown to look up in the phone book, you'd be in trouble. So would you be if you ordered a plant by mail by its common name in your community and let it go at that.

Now you know why I have listed both the botanical and common names of plants. And true to my promise, that is the only "gardenese" I'll give you. Wait. There is one other: chemicals (fertilizers, pesticides and such). Look, do you know common names for those? Don't we all go into our garden center and ask the salesman if he's got something that will kill whatever it is that makes those holes in the leaves of our pet begonia? You know you do. Now, you can do as I do. Write the chemical's name on a slip of paper and ask him for it. Watch his look of approval as he sizes you up one degree above the moron line. Ask for the product by its generic name instead of by a popular brand name, and boy, he'll really flip. Of course, keep your mouth shut afterwards unless you want to blow the whole thing. A knowing smile and a skeptical lift of the eyebrows are all you're allowed.

3

The "Good Guys" of Gardening: Trees, Shrubs, Ground Covers and Vines

Trees, shrubs, ground covers and vines are the backbone of any landscape plan, indispensable to the weekend gardener. If need be, he could have attractive gardens with these major plants and nothing else. Careful selection can provide beauty, color, texture, privacy, shade, highlights or masks for specific areas, fragrance, berries to attract birds, and a solution to erosion and other problems on steep banks. Not bad when you add that once planted and given minimum care, they continue to work for you for years and years!

Chances are you already have some of these "good guys" growing on your property. I sincerely hope, for your sake, that yours was not a house with acres of naked soil all around when you bought it for your retreat from the concrete pavements of the big city. I feel very strongly that one can always add to or alter a house (given lots of lovely money, naturally), but there are limits to what one can do insofar as handsome old trees are concerned. What is called "fast-growing" in horticultural circles is very relative indeed. We are a society used to instant gratification, and the thought of waiting ten years to have a shady nook on the terrace is not too appealing. Of course, given enough of that lovely money, one can have mature, stately trees transplanted. (There's always hope with the state lotteries.)

We will not assume that you are starting from scratch, but that more likely there are spaces on your property that need filling in, replacing or adding to—perhaps a new terrace or swimming pool that you recently had constructed needs some new plants. Whatever mistakes the previous owner may have made, there is no need for you to add your own. First of all, check to see what grows best in *your* locality. There are ways to do this quickly: look at neighboring properties, visit your local botanical garden, and see what is available at the local nurseries. You won't find coconut palms for sale in Maine. Your state Agricultural Extension Service is also an excellent source.

After you know what your area grows best, check your own grounds. No, I'm not getting too technical (whatever may be said of me, I never want to hear *that*). It's just that within a few miles, temperature, moisture and winds can vary greatly. High on a hill or deep in a valley or surrounded by thick woods can make a difference. You may even have several kinds of soil on your own property. Just check for acidity, because most trees and shrubs will be "neutral" or "acid" types. A few will definitely need an "alkaline" soil. Check your soil with one of those test kits purchased for a few dollars at the garden center and you'll find out quickly and easily.

Trees

It's safe to say that there's at least one tree to satisfy every taste and fill every need. Trees can be small (under forty feet in height), medium-sized (under seventy-five feet) and large (over seventy-five feet). Some have thick foliage (forget a lawn under those); others are light and airy, with lace-like foliage patterns. There are evergreens (keeping their leaves all year) and deciduous trees (losing leaves in winter). Some can be "semi-evergreen" in the sense that they only lose their leaves for a short period—climate is a definite factor. Some are prized for their flowers and berries, others for their graceful shape.

Let's not overlook those that have endeared themselves to our hearts because they have apparently fought and won the battle against the elements, adapting themselves to otherwise unfavorable situations such as strong, high winds (owners of penthouses and beach houses should kiss their Japanese black pines once a week), or those that don't mind "wet feet" and thrive in swamps and on river banks. There are many more, of course, and we each have our favorites. Other than an encyclopedia, there can be no really complete listing of fine trees, even limiting ourselves to those that require minimum maintenance. I wish that space could permit an illustration of each tree. Unfortunately, it doesn't. I know how annoyed I am when I read a couple of lines describing a tree, and I'm supposed to know what it looks like right now, let alone in a few years!

There's one way we can get around that. Check the list I have compiled for what seems to appeal to you. Next, look around and try to find out if any of your neighbors have what you have selected, or inquire at your best local nursery. If possible, have a look at a mature tree, and see if that is what you have in mind. You two have to "click," or else forget it. It's too much of an investment and will be with you far too long for you to settle for something that gives you only lukewarm feelings.

Know precisely what functions the tree is to perform. Shade the terrace? Screen out the neighbors? Highlight the edge of woods? Dramatize a pond? Frame the house? To reduce lawn clean-up problems, avoid trees in that area that shed flower petals, nuts, fruits or leaves. A once-a-year leaf raking around deciduous trees in the North is to be expected, but there's no need to compound the problem at other times. Place these trees where it doesn't matter what sheds where (some ground covers will swallow everything).

After you have decided on the *functions* of the tree, decide on the kind you *can* have (based on soil, climate, etc.). Finally, select the one you'd *like* to have. You can see that, by process of elimination, selecting a tree will not be such a tedious job. Yet, enough species and varieties of trees remain for you to be pretty certain of getting one that you really like.

To give just one example: you wish to screen out your neighbor's barn, which, while a distance away, nevertheless is in full view from your terrace. Evergreens are the obvious choice, as they will effectively block out that area during winter as well as the rest of the year. Staggered rows of white pines or hemlocks would be ideal. The pines are more striking, but the hemlocks have denser foliage which allows nothing to be seen through them. (Hollies are the tops, but very expensive and slow-growing.) However, you also want this screen to be a windbreak because you are in a very windy, exposed locality. This means Japanese black pine, blue spruce, Austrian pine, Scotch pine. Add the fact that you may live in a "hardiness zone" that further limits your choice to blue spruce because winter temperatures can dip to twenty below zero. Once you have made your final decision as to which tree you want, you have to decide what size to buy. Hopefully, you have a good, reliable nursery not too far away, and you are now facing *the* tree. It can be anything from a twig to a tall, handsome specimen. Naturally, the size of your nursery determines the number of varieties and amount of stock. It may be that what you want is only available in one size. But if you have a choice, let me strongly advise you to buy the largest that you can afford, and to let the nurseryman

23

plant it for you. Within a couple of years, the tree will truly resemble what you had in mind and will give you joy every time you look at it. The local nurseryman, knowing that he put it in, and that you are following his instructions (you'd better!) as to weekly watering during the summer months and into winter for the first two years, will feel a certain responsibility. Should the tree begin to look sickly, you will have an expert available to look at it and do what is necessary.

Trees of any size—certainly any with a trunk diameter of five inches or more—need several men to do a proper job of transplanting from nursery to your house, or from one part of your garden to another. Only after you have seen several strong men struggling to dig out the roots of a good-sized hemlock, burlap and tie the roots up in a ball, heave it onto the back of a truck and repeat the same procedure in reverse, planting it in a hole that looks like a crater, can you possibly understand the expertise and work involved. Not to mention the reason for the cost—which is mainly for labor. But this is *not* the time to economize. This represents a major expense that will give you years of pleasure. Have you ever walked through an old abandoned estate, left untouched for years through litigation or what not, and noticed how much of a jungle it is? It takes only two or three summers to turn flower beds into weed patches, fruits and vegetables into total disaster. But notice the trees. They couldn't care less; they go on and on and on. To a lesser degree, shrubs are a lot like that. This is why penny pinching in this area of landscaping is not wise.

Trees can do without fertilizing. If they are in or near the lawn, the fertilizer that you give the grass also will benefit the trees. Another good reason for dealing with a reputable local nurseryman is to make sure that he sells you insect- and disease-resistant varieties. This is important, and he is your best source of information, because what may be an insect-free tree in one part of the country is bugs' favorite fare in your backyard. Anyway, it's insurance against future trouble, and as long as such varieties do exist, why not avail yourself of them? If worst comes to worst, there are some excellent chemicals available to control pests. Get a tree expert to come and apply the stuff. Again, if you saw the equipment necessary to do a really thorough job, you'd wonder why anybody would want to have a go at it himself. It doesn't cost much and can be done when you're not there. Believe me, it's worth eating nothing but meatloaf for a week to have that tricky and nasty job done by a real pro.

A healthy tree can be kept that way by a few rules: (1) buy good stock from a reputable local dealer; (2) make sure it's a variety that will grow well in your general locality, and equally important, will grow well in your own garden; (3) meet the tree's culture requirements regarding dry or moist soil, acidity, sun or shade, and so on; (4) avoid any variety that is disease- or insect-prone in your area; (5) have the tree correctly planted and staked if needed; (6) follow the nurseryman's instructions as to amount of watering needed, mulching if indicated; (7) act promptly if the tree looks sickly. Call the nurseryman from whom you purchased it to see what is wrong with it, and have him do or recommend what steps it will take to correct the apparent ailment. (It may be nothing but the natural, yearly browning and shedding of needles on some pines, for instance. Or those little holes in holly leaves that used to panic me, which turned out to be nothing more than "spine spots"—wind making the leaves rub against one another, and the thorny edges naturally doing damage. It's reassuring to learn about these things—until the following winter when you've forgotten them and start worrying all over again!)

It can never be repeated too often that a listing of *anything*—plants, books, films and so on—is the equivalent of handing somebody a hefty club, sitting down calmly, and saying "Go ahead and hit me." You're not only asking for it, you're begging! But one thing must be acknowledged: if you scan enough lists, certain names will keep reappearing. If critics, scholars and experts all seem to agree on a few names out of the hundreds listed, it's safe to assume these chosen few are indeed "stars" for anyone, beginner or advanced.

In checking and cross-checking data for all lists in this book,

25

I not only have gone to one size stronger in eyeglasses, but have come to the same profound, philosophical understanding that suddenly dawns on a brand-new mother. All the books on child care, while necessary, take second place to the mother's own personal, instinctive knowledge of her baby and his needs. Similarly with this and any list of plant material: the knowledge of your own property and the surrounding area in your part of the country is the prime requisite in selecting wisely. Even if you faithfully stick to plants hardy in your zone, remember that the zone covers an enormous area, coast to coast! So please, double check anything on my list with your local nurseryman. Don't be shy about doing so. The country's top landscape architects do it all the time.

Shrubs

I will stick my neck out and say that shrubs are the most versatile and valuable plants in the garden. They are foundation plants, which is another way of saying that they soften the harsh lines of the foundation of your house (unless yours is a contemporary style with glass walls from floor to ceiling—and even then there will be certain spots that will benefit from shrubs). They provide backgrounds for flower beds. They separate, in a natural, graceful manner, one area of your property from another—such as the vegetable garden and compost pile from the flower beds, or the playground from the terrace.

Some shrubs are evergreen; others are deciduous and bloom profusely. Each category has its own special function. Shrubs come in all shapes and sizes: tall, skinny, low, wide, fast-growing, slow-growing, with flowers in spring, during summer or fall, or even in early winter and very early spring when the landscape is bare and depressing.

Many shrubs are prized for their cheerful berries or colorful foliage in autumn. A few have just about everything: flowers, berries, brilliant fall leaves, graceful growth habit, few if any maintenance requirements. These, needless to say, I have included in my list. If I have left out some all-time favorites, there is a reason. I adore lilacs—burying my face in an armful of them is sheer heaven. The gay, sunshine gold of forsythia is a very dear, welcome sign of spring. Unfortunately, for these shrubs to be at their best, they must be judiciously pruned each year. One third of the "canes" must be cut down to the ground every year to allow for a constant rejuvenation of the plant. You could let it go, but frankly, the flowers are the best part of these shrubs, and without them or with just a stingy display, they are best left for full-time gardeners.

This is not to say that other shrubs can be left alone forever, but there is a difference between a once-in-a-while thinning out, chiefly for dead or diseased wood, and a regular schedule. It is the difference between "you must do it" and "if you have the time and inclination, it might be a good idea." Someone pressed for time would appreciate this distinction.

For the same reason, I have not included a list of shrubs for "hedges." Any shrubs, if planted thickly in a row, become a natural hedge. The minute one has to start clipping and shearing, time-consuming work results—and not always for the better. Allowing shrubs to grow their own way is—to me anyway—far more beautiful than turning them into geometric patterns. By selecting those shrubs which grow only to a certain height, one can have just the right size hedge needed.

As with annuals and perennials, it is best if you restrict yourself to a few kinds of shrubs, using these generously. One or two of everything will give your garden a nursery look. Instead, visualize an entire bank of mountain laurel in bloom in the spring, keeping its handsome green leaves throughout winter—or a cluster of viburnums, a mass of white flowers in late May, covered with berries (and birds) in the fall! The beauty of shrubs is that they vary so much in color, texture, shape and size that not many different kinds are needed to give variety to the garden.

As with trees, shrubs are a serious and expensive investment. Give careful thought to the function and overall design of your garden plan before buying any. Evergreens are a must for those who live in colder northern climates. There is no need to have a bare landscape in winter, thanks to them. Would snow be as beautiful if it were not seen shining brilliantly in the sun on top of junipers? Decide first of all *why* you need shrubs and *where*. Then select according to your zone, soil type, sun or shade, etc. Flowering shrubs are usually light and airy, making a superb contrast to the sturdy evergreens. What you are really doing is painting a canvas. Your imagination and ability to visualize are essential for pleasing results. The shrub you buy today may be three times wider and taller in a year or two. Think of that and leave space accordingly. I have given minimum and maximum height and spread of each shrub, but somewhere between is realistic. A plant reaches its maximum size when it is grown under ideal conditions. Hemlocks can reach two hundred feet—but growing wild, in the forests. This is why people who buy land first, and then build a house, have it made: "instant landscaping" followed by leisurely home building!

If you meet the culture requirements of a shrub and plant it properly there is no reason why it should give you any trouble. I left out those that are known to be disease- or insect-prone or delicate, however beautiful they may be. Of course, each year new and stronger varieties are introduced, so here again, your nurseryman is your best friend.

Ground Covers

Ground covers do a great deal more than provide a "carpet of green" around the house. After all, grass does that too. Ground covers are low plants, either evergreen or deciduous, which spread quickly to form a dense cover for the ground. Many people only

28

think in terms of using ground covers where grass does not grow well. This is a good reason, but far from the only one. Obviously, grass will not grow under dense shade or in poor soil. Even where it will grow well, use of a lawn mower may be extremely difficult. Solution: a ground cover. However, here are some other uses: rock gardens, natural woodland gardens, a steep bank to prevent soil erosion, along paths, beside steps, at the base of trees, anywhere that hand-trimming a lawn would be needed. This cuts down maintenance. Ground covers also "tie" together shrubs and specimen plants. The restful green carpeting is a perfect base or platform for many plants.

There are hundreds of plants which can be used as ground covers. They can be low enough to fit between stepping stones or bricks, or they can form a carpet two feet high, but the majority are under twelve inches. They add texture to the ground, some flowering, others having berries. Best of all, they require practically no maintenance.

If cultural requirements are followed and the right plant is chosen for the right place, planting should be the end of it. At the beginning, there will be need for watering, weeding (not too much if a thick mulch is applied), and fertilizing. Once established, with the plants reaching toward one another and merging to form the thick carpeting, it's on its own. And you're sitting down doing nothing. Hallelujah! The initial cost may seem high when compared to grass seed, but believe me, it's more than worth it. Besides, don't be fooled into thinking that a good lawn can't run up impressive bills!

A good ground cover obviously should be attractive, but it should also be winter hardy in your area. If you have to cover it with salt hay in the winter to prevent heaving by frost action—and semi-hardy types need this care—forget it. Anyway, you won't find them on my list.

Start by preparing the ground well—the way you would for any planting. Add peat moss and commercial fertilizer to the soil. A good fertilizer is a combination of any 5-10-5, applied at the rate of about three pounds per hundred square feet. Before planting

29

the ground cover, remove existing weeds by using special chemicals made for that purpose. How closely you space the plants depends on your budget and/or patience. It also depends on how quickly the plants grow, on their size at time of purchase and size when fully mature. A rule of thumb is one plant for every one to four square feet. In areas where you can expect leaves dropping each fall, choose a ground cover that will "swallow" leaves, enriching the soil as a bonus.

Note the *location* of your ground covers, because some thrive in shade, others in full sun. Don't worry if you have dry, sandy soil, or if it's moist and wet. There's a ground cover for each type. As already mentioned, you can even have some that flower, have berries, and are fragrant. Now, can you ask for more? If you want to, you can set your lawn mower on a slab of marble rising out of the ground cover and call it pop art, because you don't ever have to use it again if you choose not to.

I guess by now you get the message that I'm sold on ground covers. If diamonds are a girl's best friend, and a dog a man's best friend, then I might as well add my own cliché and say that the ground cover is the reluctant weekend gardener's best friend.

One more word of praise, and I'll stop. If your ground is uneven, in the sense that you have little dips here and there, grass will show up these miniature hills and valleys. But a ground cover will hide them, simply because its height and texture will make these "potholes" disappear.

It has taken enormous self-control on my part to dwindle the list of ground covers to a mere handful. I have concentrated on the hardiest and easiest to obtain. The latter is important because ground covers are bought in fairly large quantities, not likely to be mail-ordered. The gardener generally is dependent on his local nursery. That's good, from the point of view that only those that will "make it" in his area are going to be for sale; but it's bad in that some very fine plants, equally suitable, are bypassed because they are not available. But why should I tempt you with something you might not be able to obtain? One look at the list, however, should calm any fears. These ground covers are all stars—be assured of that. If some that are not listed are available in your locality, then by all means consider them.

Vines

There is a bit of overlapping between a ground cover and a vine. They both "spread" and "creep," but how and where make the difference. Anything that spreads over the soil and covers it, as far as I'm concerned, is treated as a ground cover. Once it starts growing upwards, reaching for the sky, or falls over walls or dangles from window boxes, it becomes a vine.

English ivy is probably the star example of versatility personified. It's a ground cover, and it's also a vine because it grows up (on walls) or down (from window boxes, hanging baskets or planters). There are so many varieties of ivy that no one will attempt to give a total figure. Some have leaves shaped like hearts (named "238th Street" because it was developed at the New York Botanical Garden located nearby), others have ruffled leaves ("Fluffy Ruffles"), some have leaves with five lobes in all sizes (from tiny "Walthamensis" to giant "Bulgaria," five inches across). You can have leaves that are shaped like bird tracks in the snow or like arrowheads. Colors vary enormously, from pale to deep green, yellow or chartreuse, with white edges that turn rosy in cold weather. And you thought you knew what ivy looked like, did you? I also thought of it as an old workhorse, good where nothing else would grow. Well, the "ivy league" has changed in lots of ways!

It is essential, indeed crucial, to know how a vine climbs. Some will do it beautifully of their own accord, without any assist from you, while others are downright lazy and need your help, encouragement and support. By support, I don't mean the moral kind; I mean good, sturdy wooden posts and trellises. The weight of these vines at maturity, and battering by winter winds, can have the whole business tumbling down or leaning like the tower of Pisa. Unfortunately, the kind of support you buy readymade at garden centers is rarely substantial enough. It may look graceful, but it has no real strength, at least not once some vines have got their hooks into it! You guessed it: this means having to build these supports yourself. This also means forget it, unless the support already exists, such as a wire or wooden fence. But you will still have to train the vine to go where you want it by tying it to the support as it goes along.

The lazy gardener is lucky that there are so many handsome "independent workers" among vines from which he can choose. Those that come with their own built-in "adhesive discs" and cling tenaciously to anything within reach are for you and me. Also, as with ground covers, only those that are winter hardy in your locality should be selected.

Vines can be put to many uses. They break up the monotony of large, solid wall surfaces. When fences have to be erected for safety reasons (as around a swimming pool) or to indicate boundary lines of the property, their harshness can be softened by vines, and what was an eyesore can become an attractive asset. Also, let's admit it, not all houses are architectural gems. Weekend retreats are more likely to be purchased for their location and the beauty of the surrounding landscape than for the looks of the houses. Here is where vines can mask exposed pipes, cover old chimneys, give charm to an ordinary-looking garage. Give some thought to *why* you want to use the vine.

The cultivation of vines is relatively easy, because most of them are such rapid growers (bless them) they don't need fertilizers, unless you want to cover a silo. Plant the vine in good soil, in the right spot, in a large enough hole, and water and mulch to keep out weeds; that's about it. When it gets too exhuberant, just give it a haircut—unless you want it to pop through a crack and start growing inside the living room wall. The ivy on my garage wall started going *under* it, and began its merry way along the inside. Just for fun, I'm letting it go, but enough's enough. When I can no longer distinguish the tools hanging on the garage walls, I'll call a halt and turn into a barber.

Annual vines are quick-growing and frequently produce lovely flowers (like Morning Glory). But honestly now, when you can get a handsome perennial that will keep on growing, repeat its flowering cycle each year, and your work is finished with planting . . . wouldn't you select that one? My chapter on annuals certainly proves that I am one of their ardent admirers, but when it comes to vines, I give my vote to perennials.

DECIDUOUS TREES

BOTANICAL NAME	COMMON NAME	HEIGHT	SPREAD	HARDINESS ZONE (SOUTHWARD)	BLOOMING SEASON	REMARKS
Acer Negundo	Box-Elder Maple	40'-70'	20'-35'	2		For western states only. Withstands drought, wind. Rapid grower.
Acer Palmatum	Japanese Maple	10'-25'	8'-20'	4		Superb specimen tree. Graceful, delicate, colorful leaves.
Acer Saccharum	Sugar Maple	75'-125'	50'-100'	3		Long-lived, stately tree. Magnificent fall color.
Betula Papyrifera	Canoe or Paper Birch	40'-80'	15'-25'	5 northward to Arctic		Striking white bark peels off like paper. Graceful branches. Dramatic in front of evergreens. Likes acid soil. Not for the southern states.
Cornus Florida	Flowering Dogwood	20'-30'	12'-18'	5	Spring	White flowers. Variety "rubra" has pink flowers. Berries in fall. Likes acid soil, part shade. Ideal at edge of woodland, under taller trees.
Crataegus Phaenopyrum	Washington Thorn	20'-30'	12'-15'	4	Early Summer	White flowers. Red berries and colorful foliage. Handsome specimen for all seasons. Full sun. Tolerates alkaline soil and drought.
Elaeagnus Angustifolia	Russian Olive	10'-20'	5'-10'	2		Hardy to below 35°. Wind resistant. Good for Prairie states and seashore. Likes dry areas. Willowy silver foliage. Whitish, fragrant flowers. Yellow fruit.
Fagus Sylvatica	European Beech	80'-100'	50'-70'	4		Stately specimen tree. Provides dense shade. Needs lots of room. Good drainage essential.

DECIDUOUS TREES (cont.)

BOTANICAL NAME	COMMON NAME	HEIGHT	SPREAD	HARDINESS ZONE (SOUTHWARD)	BLOOMING SEASON	REMARKS
Fraxinus Pensylvanica Lanceolata	Green Ash	40'-70'	30'-60'	3		Vigorous shade tree. Useful in dry, wind-swept areas.
Ginkgo Biloba	Maidenhair Tree	100'-125'	20'-25'	5 northward		Attractive growth habit. Withstands wind and will grow well anywhere. Use male plant only.
Gleditsia Triacanthos	Honey Locust	70'-130'	25'-50'	4		Lacy foliage. Great for light shade. Use thornless variety only. Likes alkaline soil. Withstands drought, sun, smoke.
Liquidambab Styraciflua	Sweet Gum	70'-120'	40'-80'	4		Gorgeous fall coloring and symmetry. Will tolerate seashore. Best in full sun and moist location.
Malus Floribunda	Japanese Flowering Crab-Apple	15'-25'	10'-20'	4	Spring	A mass of flowers in spring and bright fruit in fall. Likes alkaline soil.
Quercus Balustris	Pin Oak	80'-90'	30'-40'	4		One of the best and fastest growing oaks. Symmetrical, pyramidal head. Tolerates more moisture than other oaks. Likes acid soil.
Sophora Japonica	Pagoda Tree	40'-60'	30'-60'	4	Summer	Handsome, rounded, full tree.
Zelkova Serrata	Japanese Zelkova	50'-80'	50'-80'	4		The best substitute for those who like the elm. Same graceful growth habit, resistant to Dutch elm disease.

EVERGREEN TREES

BOTANICAL NAME	COMMON NAME	HEIGHT	SPREAD	HARDINESS ZONE (SOUTHWARD)	REMARKS
Abies Concolor	White Fir	75'-125'	25'-50'	4	Excellent accent tree. Light, sandy loam. Good drainage essential.
Cedrus Libani	Cedar of Lebanon	60'-100'	60'-100'	5	Handsome specimen. Needs lots of room to spread. Not for Prairie states. Good for seashore. Not too much moisture.
Cryptomeria Japonica	Japanese Cryptomeria	40'-125'	12'-40'	6	Pyramidal. Good for hedge or screen. Full sun, no wind.
Ilex Opaca	American Holly	10'-50'	5'-25'	5	Magnificent as specimen. Slow grower. Red berries. Likes acid soil. Not for Prairie states or windy locations.
Juniperus Virginiana	Red Cedar	40'-80'	8'-12'	2	Fragrant foliage. Pyramid shape. Good for background or screen. Bluish berries.
Picea Pungens	Colorado Blue Spruce	80'-140'	30'-50'	2	Use for accent. Sandy loam, acid lover. Good drainage essential. Does not like windy site.
Pinus Strobus	White Pine	90'-150'	30'-50'	3	Sandy loam. Avoid too much moisture. Acid lover. Excellent tree for specimen and screening. One of the most beautiful and graceful evergreens.
Pinus Sylvestris	Scotch Pine	40'-75'	15'-25'	3	Picturesque growth habit. Likes wind, excellent as windbreak. Any soil.
Pinus Thunbergi	Japanese Black Pine	100'-125'	50'-65'	4	Picturesque. Good for seashore as it likes wind. Excellent in Japanese gardens.
Tsuga Canadensis	Canada (Common) Hemlock	40'-90'	20'-45'	3	Beautiful evergreen excellent for screening, as hedge, as background. Thick, dense, fast growing. Shade or sun.

DECIExtDUOUS SHRUBS

DECIDUOUS SHRUBS

BOTANICAL NAME	COMMON NAME	HEIGHT	SPREAD	HARDINESS ZONE (SOUTHWARD)	BLOOMING SEASON	REMARKS
Abelia Grandiflora	Glossy Abelia	4'-6'	4'-6'	6	Summer	Semi-evergreen. Small, shiny leaves. Sun or light shade. Pink or white flowers.
Azalea Calendulacea	Flame Azalea	6'-12'	4'-8'	5	May-June	Plant in mass. Needs acid soil and mulch. Light shade. Yellow, orange, red flowers.
Azalea Mollis	Mollis Azalea (Chinese Azalea)	5'-6'	4'-5'	6	May or June	Mass planting best. Does not mind type of soil. Yellow, orange, reddish flowers.
Azalea Nudiflora	Pinkster Flower Azalea	4'-6'	3'-5'	5	May	Pink or white flowers. Fragrant.
Azalea Viscosa	Swamp Azalea	6'-10'	4'-8'	4 to 6 only	June or July	Very fragrant white flowers. Needs low, moist location.
Berberis Thunbergi (several varieties)	Japanese Barberry	4'-6'	4'-6'	4	May	Yellow flowers. Red berries well into winter. Spines on branches make it good as protective hedges.

DECIDUOUS SHRUBS (cont.)

BOTANICAL NAME	COMMON NAME	HEIGHT	SPREAD	HARDINESS ZONE (SOUTHWARD)	BLOOMING SEASON	REMARKS
Buddleia Davidi	Butterfly-Bush or Summer Lilac	4'-10'	3'-8'	6 (in 4 and 5 will be winter-killed but will bloom next year)	July to frost	Fragrant "lilac" flowers. Full sun. Rich soil. Beautiful shrub near terraces.
Clethra Alnifolia	Sweet Pepperbush	3'-9'	2'-7'	3	August-September	Very fragrant flowers, white or pink. Does well in full sun and ordinary soil, but prefers light shade and moist soil.
Cotoneaster Divaricata	Spreading Cotoneaster	4'-6'	4'-6'	5	Spring	Small pink flowers, bright red berries and dark purple foliage in fall. Good border shrub for shady site.
Elaeagnus Commutata	Wolfberry or Silverberry	8'-12'	8'-12'	2	May-July	Silvery leaves and fruit. Fragrant yellow flowers. Hardy to -50°.

DECIADUOUS SHRUBS (cont.)

BOTANICAL NAME	COMMON NAME	HEIGHT	SPREAD	HARDINESS ZONE (SOUTHWARD)	BLOOMING SEASON	REMARKS
Eleagnus Multiflora	Cherry Eleagnus (Gumi)	4'-9'	3'-8'	4	May	Silvery leaves and fruit. Bright red fruit in fall.
Euonymus Alatus Compacta	Winged Spindle-tree or Flame Bush	5'-6'	4'-5'	4	Negligible	Brilliant scarlet fruit and leaves in autumn. Fabulous placed near evergreens.
Hamamelis Vernalis	Vernal Witch-hazel	4'-8'	2'-4'	5	January thru March	Yellow flowers. Easily grown. Good accent in winter landscape.
Hamamelis Virginiana	Native Witch-hazel	8'-15'	6'-12'	3	October or November	Bright yellow flowers when everything else has stopped blooming.
Hydrangea Macrophylla	Hortensia	3'-6'	3'-6'	5	Summer	Globe-shaped clusters of pink or blue flowers.
Hypericum Moserianum	St. John's-wort Goldflower	1'-3'	1'-3'	6	June thru September	Good for front of shrub border. Yellow flowers.

DECIDUOUS SHRUBS (cont.)

BOTANICAL NAME	COMMON NAME	HEIGHT	SPREAD	HARDINESS ZONE (SOUTHWARD)	BLOOMING SEASON	REMARKS
Kolkwitzia Amabilis	*Beauty-Bush*	5'-10'	3-8'	4	June	Pink flowers. Full sun, spectacular shrub for background.
Myrica Pensylvanica	*Bayberry*	3'-8'	4'-7'	2		Aromatic foliage. Likes sandy soil and exposed dry locations. Great for seashore.
Rosa Rugosa	*Rugosa Rose*	4'-6'	4'-6'	4	July and August	Red or white flowers. Large orange-red fruit in fall. Loves seashore and dry, sandy, exposed windy location.
Viburnum Tomentosum	*Double-File Viburnum*	7'-10'	6'-8'	4	May-June	Lovely white flowers. Follows dogwood in blooming. Red fruit in fall attracts birds. Symmetrical arrangement of flowers along horizontal branches. Truly beautiful and striking bush.

EVERGREEN SHRUBS

BOTANICAL NAME	COMMON NAME	HEIGHT	SPREAD	HARDINESS ZONE (SOUTHWARD)	REMARKS
Euonymus (Epatens) Kiautschovicus	Spreading Euonymus	4'-7'	3'-6'	6	Beautiful foliage.
Ilex Crenata	Japanese Holly	2'-20' according to variety	2'-10'	5	Superb shrub. Best 3 varieties: convexa, microphylla (very hardy) and latifolia. The latter makes the finest of all hedges.
Juniperus Chinensis Pfitzeriana	Pfitzer's Juniper	4'-10'	5'-8'	3	Partly upright, spreading branches forming hollow in center. Tolerates dry, windy location. Good for seashore. Full sun.
Juniperus Sabina	Savin Juniper	4'-5'	4'-5'	4	Medium height, upright juniper. Dry, sunny location. Does not like acid soil.
Kalmia Latifolia	Mountain Laurel	4'-10'	4'-10'	4	Superb, broad-leaf shrub with lovely pinkish flowers in spring. Must have acid soil. Best for naturalized plantings. Semi-shade or sun.
Pieris Japonica	Japanese Pieris (Andromeda)	3'-10'	4'-8'	5	Handsome shrub for foundation planting. Likes slightly acid soil, shelter from wind. Pieris floribunda is smaller shrub and hardy from zone 4 southward.

EVERGREEN SHRUBS (cont.)

BOTANICAL NAME	COMMON NAME	HEIGHT	SPREAD	HARDINESS ZONE (SOUTHWARD)	REMARKS
Pyracantha Coccinea Lalandi	Laland's Firethorn	12'-20'	6'	5 (4 if sheltered in warm spot)	White flowers in early summer, fabulous orange berries in fall. Neutral or slightly alkaline soil. Excellent as a hedge or against a wall.
Rhododendron Carolinianum	Carolina Rhododendron	4'-6'	4'-6'	4	Superb broad-leaf shrub. Rose-purplish flowers in spring. Compact growth. Full sun, but not for hot, coastal plain.
Rhododendron Maximum	Rosebay Rhododendron (or Great Laurel)	10'-25'	8'-20'	4 to 6 only	Great shrub for tall background or screening. Likes shade.
Rhododendron Wilsoni	Wilson Rhododendron	6'-8'	3'-5'	4 to 6 only	Low, compact. Droops over wall. Good as foreground of larger rhododendrons.
Taxus Cuspidata Nana	Dwarf Japanese Yew	4'-6'	4'-6'	4 (3 if protected)	Hardier, easier to grow than English yew and just as handsome.
Taxus Media Hicksi	Japanese Hicks Yew	15'-20'	3'-4'	4	Upright, dense shrub. Narrow, excellent for hedges.

DECIDUOUS AND EVERGREEN GROUND COVERS

BOTANICAL NAME	COMMON NAME	HEIGHT	HARDINESS ZONE (SOUTHWARD)	SITE	FLOWER COLOR	BLOOM PERIOD	REMARKS
Ajuga (Varieties)	Bugleweed	4"-10"	5	Sun or shade	Tall blue, white or pink spikes	May-June	Fast grower. Will spread right into lawn, but can be mowed. Semi-evergreen.
Artosta-phylos Uva-ursi	Bearberry	6"-12"	3	Sandy soil, dry exposed location			Red stems and berries. Good for seashore. Evergreen.
Cotoneaster Horizontalis	Rock Cotoneaster	18"-24"	5	Sun, slightly alkaline soil, well-drained	Pinkish	May	Red berries into December. Semi-evergreen.
Cotoneaster Microphylla	Rock Spray	24"-36"	5	Same as above	White, profuse	May-June	Numerous red berries right into March. Great over banks and walls. Evergreen.
Euonymus Fortunei Coloratus	Winter-creeper	6"-12"	4	Sun, will tolerate shade	Greenish-white	May-June	Purple-red foliage during winter. Evergreen.

DECIDUOUS AND EVERGREEN GROUND COVERS (cont.)

BOTANICAL NAME	COMMON NAME	HEIGHT	HARDINESS ZONE (SOUTHWARD)	SITE	FLOWER COLOR	BLOOM PERIOD	REMARKS
Hedera Helix	English Ivy	4"-10"	5 (4 if protected)	Sun or shade, but prefers shade			Spreads rapidly. Great with bulbs. Baltica best variety. Evergreen.
Juniperus Horizontalis Varieties: Douglasi Bar Harbor Plumosa	Creeping Juniper Varieties: Waukegan Bar Harbor Andorra	6"-12"	2	Sun, sandy rocky soil			Blue fruit. Very versatile and valuable ground cover. Evergreen.
Lonicera Japonica Halliana	Hall's Honeysuckle	4"-10"	4	Sun or shade, slightly moist soil	White, fragrant	Summer	A quick way to cover a bank or steep slope. Must be used where it can't take over nearby flower beds or shrubs. Semi-evergreen.
Mahonia Repens	Creeping Barberry	12"	4	Partial shade	Yellow	All summer	Small black fruit in fall. Evergreen.
Pachysandra Terminalis	Japanese Spurge	6"-8"	5	Shade or sun, but prefers shade	White	May-June	Spreads rapidly—even into lawn, but can be mowed down. Handsome, shiny leaves. Excellent with bulbs. Evergreen.

DECIDUOUS AND EVERGREEN GROUND COVERS (cont.)

BOTANICAL NAME	COMMON NAME	HEIGHT	HARDINESS ZONE (SOUTHWARD)	SITE	FLOWER COLOR	BLOOM PERIOD	REMARKS
Rosa Rugosa Max Graf	Shrub Rose	24"-30"	4	Sun or part shade, sandy soil	Deep pink	July-August	Excellent for seashore, will quickly cover a bank or slope. Deciduous.
Thymus Serpyllum (Varieties)	Mother-of-Thyme, Creeping Thyme	1"-3"	4	Sun or shade, dry soil	Purple or Red	Summer	Spreading mat, excellent for in-between stepping stones. Very fragrant foliage. Evergreen.
Vaccinium Angustifolium	Low Bush Blueberry	12"-18"	3	Sun or shade, stands heat & dryness	White	April-May	Blue-black fruit. Deciduous.
Vaccinium Pensylvanicum	Dwarf Blueberry	10"-12"	3	Same as above	White	April-May	Blue-black fruit. Deciduous.
Vinca Minor	Periwinkle or Myrtle	6"-8"	5	Sun or shade	Bright blue	May	Shiny leaves. Clumps soon form thick mat. Evergreen.

DECIDUOUS VINES

BOTANICAL NAME	COMMON NAME	HEIGHT	HARDINESS ZONE (SOUTHWARD)	SITE	FLOWER COLOR	BLOOM PERIOD	REMARKS
Celastrus Orbiculatus	Oriental Bittersweet	20'-30'	5	Sun or shade			Requires additional support. Vigorous grower. Numerous yellow-orange fruit. Watch for infective scale like that of Euonymus.
Celastrus Scandens	American Bittersweet	8'-10'	3	Sun or shade			Good for covering low walls as it stays neat and shrubby. Yellow fruit.
Clematis (Hybrids)	Clematis	8'-12'	3	Likes lime, cool roots, "head" in sun	White, pinks, purples, violets. Large flowers	July thru October	Florida or patens are hybrids to look for, as they bloom on old wood and require practically no pruning, but require support to climb.
Clematis Paniculata (and other wild species)	Japanese Clematis	20'-30'	4	Same as above	White, fragrant. Small flowers	Fall	Needs additional support. Use over fences and lattices to make it easier.
Hydrangea Petiolaris	Climbing Hydrangea	30'-50'	4		White		Train when young. Clings to masonry or brick or tree trunks.

DECIDUOUS VINES (cont.)

BOTANICAL NAME	COMMON NAME	HEIGHT	HARDINESS ZONE (SOUTHWARD)	SITE	FLOWER COLOR	BLOOM PERIOD	REMARKS
Lonicera Periclymenum	Honeysuckle, Twisted Eglantine	10'-20'	4	Any soil, but prefers slightly moist	Yellowish-white, fragrant	June thru August	Red fruit in August and September. Birds love it. Give it plenty of room, let it roam and forget it!
Parthenocissus Quinquefolia Engelmannii (Ampelopsis Quinquefolia)	Virginia Creeper	50'-90'	3	Sun or shade, any soil			Striking scarlet leaves in fall. Excellent for woodland areas, walls, naturalistic slopes. Rampant grower.
Polygonum Aubertii	Silver-Lace Vine	15'-30'	4	Sun or part shade	White, fragrant, profuse	August	Excellent as "tumbler" over walls. Attracts bees. Rampant grower. Needs support to climb—and severe pruning, if space is limited.
Wistaria Floribunda (or Sinensis-Chinese Wisteria)	Japanese Wisteria	20'-50'	4	Sun, average soil	Violet-blue, fragrant	May	If you have any old, dying tree, plant a wisteria at its base. All wisterias need guidance the first year. After that, it's on its own! Keep away from house, needs too much pruning.

EVERGREEN VINES

BOTANICAL NAME	COMMON NAME	HEIGHT	HARDINESS ZONE (SOUTHWARD)	SITE	FLOWER COLOR	BLOOM PERIOD	REMARKS
Clematis Armandii	Clematis	10'-15'	7	Cool, moist, well drained soil, likes lime	White	May	Mostly for California or similar climate.
Euonymus Fortunei Acutus	Sharp-leaf Wintercreeper	6'-10'	4	Sun or part shade	Greenish-white	May-June	Small leaves, good climber. Pale pink fruit. Excellent vine, but in some parts of country, susceptible to Euonymus scale. Forget it in this case.
Hedera Helix Baltica	English Ivy	50'-90'	4 (if protected 5)	Prefers shade, well drained soil	White (inconspicuous)	July	Needs some protection from winter sun.
Lonicera Sempervirens	Trumpet Honeysuckle	20'-30'	4	Slightly moist soil	Orange or red	May to August	Evergreen in mild climates only. Rampant grower. Give it plenty of room. Orange-scarlet fruit.
Parthenocissus Tricuspidata (Ampelopsis Tricuspidata)	Boston Ivy	50'-90'	4	Sun or shade			Hardier than English Ivy.

4

That Casual Affair with Annuals: The Spice in Your Garden

If annuals didn't already exist, somebody would have to invent them just for the part-time gardener. Of course, even the dedicated, full-time gardener appreciates these hard-working plants. And why not? They bloom all summer long, creating a riot of colors in the garden, precisely at the time of year one lives outdoors the most, entertaining friends for weekends, enjoying those extra-long days while they last. True, in the spring, when the trees are still bare and the wind hasn't yet lost its bite, it's great for the owner's morale to see those gay flowering bulbs pop out of the ground; the same goes for autumn-flowering plants.

But it is during the summer months that weekenders most enjoy their retreat. They have outdoor parties, barbecues, city friends dropping hints for invitations. This is the moment of truth for the lazy gardener. He wants "instant gratification" from his garden, and that means annuals to the rescue, as most perennials are past their flowering peak by late July and August.

To ignore annuals because they are born and die within one season and must be planted anew each year is to overlook the fact that many of our favorite perennials must be dug up, divided, and replanted every year or so if maximum quality and quantity of flowers are to be obtained. Annuals are planted after the last frost in spring, and are killed by the first frost in fall. Therefore, they are shallow-rooted since they need to draw nourishment from the soil for only a few months. This enables them to be planted on top of bulbs (replacing dead foliage) or near them, if you are the nervous type like I am. They can fill out the flower bed, tucked in here and there where perennials and shrubs cannot survive.

Annuals are at their most spectacular when massed in one area, or cascading from window boxes or overflowing tubs and planters, for they are lush plants, generous with their flowers. Because their lifespan is limited to a single season, their instinct is to reproduce frantically. A bit poignant, don't you think? For this reason, the more they are cut, the more they bloom. The majority require plenty of water and sun, but some of the most beautiful ones thrive in the shade.

Watering annuals thoroughly once a week should be enough (because you've been wise and put down a nice, deep mulch all around them). How much water is "enough" can be determined by checking to see if the soil is moist down to the roots, not merely on the surface. Time it to see how long it takes your sprinkler to do this and stick to a weekly schedule. Soaker hoses are even better than sprinklers, as they don't wet the foliage, but you must angle them properly to make certain you've "covered" all the plants.

Adding a mulch to flower beds, as well as to window boxes and planters, not only helps to retain moisture in the soil, but keeps the weeds down. But do make it thick enough. If you can see patches of soil, it's useless. Weeds will take over. To be effective, a mulch should be three to four inches thick. You needn't waste it, either. After the annuals have been hit by the first frost, simply pull them out, rake the mulch smooth, and the bed is ready for next spring. Also, it looks a lot neater and more attractive than would plain soil during the winter months. Come spring, rake it onto a sheet of plastic or burlap, plant the new annuals, put back the mulch (with a bit more added) and away you go.

A word of caution: when the term "shade" is used, as opposed to "sun," it doesn't mean total or dense shade where even an occasional ray of sunlight doesn't filter through. Annuals will not grow there, nor will any other flowering plant for that matter. If your outdoor area is so thickly wooded that you find yourself without a spot for even the smallest flower bed, consider judicious and careful thinning of a tree or two (done by professionals only). This will allow enough light for you to have some shade-loving plants. Plant sun-loving ones in containers around your terrace.

Annuals are lenient about soil requirements. They are not nearly as fussy as other plants; ordinary garden soil will do for most. I won't kid you, if come spring you shoot some "vitamins" into the soil, you may be rewarded with a bigger show of flowers. This simply means adding some peat moss and/or dehydrated cow manure to the soil. This is sufficient. Too much fertilizing of annuals can result in great foliage and few flowers, or burning of the shallow roots. Of course, adequate drainage is important, as is the acidity of the soil. It's not difficult to check drainage. Dig a hole about eight to ten inches deep, and fill it with water. The next day, fill it again with water and see how long the water stays there. If it drains away in eight hours, you're doing fine. If not, better locate your flower bed elsewhere, or raise the soil level by adding more soil which will provide drainage. Surround this "raised bed" with a wooden or masonry wall, or flat natural rocks. This is not only for the sake of appearance, but to prevent the formation of gullies during heavy rains.

If you have reason to feel that your soil is excessively acid or alkaline, then by all means test it with one of those kits sold at

51

garden supply stores. Limestone will sweeten your soil if it's too acid, and iron sulfate will improve it if it's too alkaline. Complete directions come with these products, so do read them carefully.

It's good to remember that proper spacing is essential to the full development of the plant, but don't overdo it if you want a lush, rich-looking flower bed. These annuals will be there only for a few months, so, unlike with shrubs or perennials, you can exercise a bit of wild abandon. Not all annuals out of the same flat will grow to the same height or width. A few won't make it. Insure yourself against this by planting enough to compensate for a "hole" here and there. You can always transplant one from a too crowded area to where the growth is spindly and sort of blah looking. If possible, buy plants that are already growing in peat pots. You put plant and pot in the hole and you're finished. Some are grown right in the flats, so all you do is gently break away each one from the rest like a batch of brownies. Firm the soil around each plant and then water deeply. Add mulch, and then sit back and enjoy the whole thing for the rest of the summer—except for watering, as already mentioned.

It's really up to you if you want to remove faded flowers and seed pods. This is desirable, no doubt about it, as it maintains vigorous growth of the plants, but it is a nuisance to do. For that matter, all flowering plants benefit from this periodic haircut, as well as shrubs such as rhododendrons. If your flower bed is small enough and you're in the mood, pick up a pair of scissors and go zipping along. I've grown lantanas that were real shrubs in height and width, with literally hundreds of flowers on each one. Cutting off the faded flowers before they could turn into seed pods became such a time-consuming chore that I limited my "haircut" routine to the parts of the plant that were most visible, leaving the rest to go nature's way.

Choosing the right annuals for your garden can take time if you dwell too long on the awesome thought that each genus can have hundreds of species, which in turn can have thousands of varieties. By using a "survival of the fittest" approach, I limited myself to forty "champions" which passed the test; they are listed at the end of the chapter. It is no coincidence that these are also the most popular. Gardeners, especially the full-time, dedicated ones, will take the time and trouble to coddle and pamper a shrub or a perennial, feeling that eventually they will be amply rewarded, but no such patience is lavished on annuals, whose season to "produce or else" is so short. By "short," I mean compared to other plants which live on for years. Annuals have by no means a short blooming season. I don't consider "short" a flowering period which begins a couple of weeks after the plant is put in the ground and goes on all through summer and fall.

Which annuals are available to the part-time gardener boils down to what is stocked by his local nursery. Most have a good selection, so that there is usually little reason to send away for annuals from a mail-order firm, unless you want a particular plant and are unable to get it. If you can't obtain it, check first whether it's simply that your local nursery doesn't choose to carry it, or whether it happens to be an annual which won't grow well in your part of the country. This is important. There may be a good reason why you cannot buy it. Look into it first.

Actually, you won't need many different kinds of annuals. For effect and good design, you want a sizeable number of the same variety to create a "splash" or mass effect, rather than a couple of this and a couple of that. Therefore, select carefully as to height and color, and go all out on a few.

Don't be tempted to grow annuals—or anything else—from seed. Like baking bread, it is soul-satisfying, creative, and makes you feel like a real "pro." Also, it's inexpensive. But let me state strongly that this is *not* for the weekend gardener. Sowing seeds on a Sunday and not going near them until the following Saturday is playing horticultural Russian roulette. Constant moisture is the key, and this requires daily attention. Too little dries out the seeds, while too much causes them to rot. A few will make it, but it isn't worth the bother.

And there is still the thinning out to be done later. This can

53

only be compared to plucking your eyebrows. It's a delicate affair, which can drive you to that third martini you said you never would have. Out of what appear to be hundreds of tiny sprouts, you have to pick a couple of dozen "sturdy" ones as winners, giving all the others the ax, so to speak. This takes will power! Those you keep you will still have to nurse along, praying that you don't get any heavy rain. So save your pennies another way, and buy healthy, growing young plants from your nursery. Some already will be in bloom, so you'll know just the color scheme you'll get—a great advantage, believe me.

Short of painting a lawn green and sticking artificial flowers in it, I can't think of any easier way of obtaining summer-long color than through annuals. Each year seems to bring a new crop of dazzlers. Horticulturists are constantly at work improving breeds, making plants disease-free, creating dwarf varieties where none existed before, mixing colors that would be the envy of Impressionists. For this reason, selecting annuals at random can create problems later, if certain factors are not taken into consideration. Consulting my chart before making your list will prevent you from choosing a plant that will grow three feet tall when you wanted something low to edge a border. Some trail and are great for hanging baskets. Those with fragrance are delightful near a terrace, when their perfume is heightened at twilight.

If you wish a blue and white color combination, for instance, go down the appropriate columns on the chart and make your choice *after* you have checked other requirements such as light and soil. Keep sun-loving plants together and shade-loving ones in their own corner. There is a certain amount of leeway. You will note that some annuals do well in both sun and partial shade. This could be the answer for a flower bed which is partly under a tree and partly in full sun. In short, there is something suitable for every corner of your property (except dense shade, of course).

What to avoid? A hodge-podge of colors, heights, shapes. Multicolored or brilliant flowers can be set off with white ones in between. This has a calming effect, yet focuses attention on the showy plants.

Those with colorful foliage also can be treated this way. A bed of coleus with its brilliantly colored leaves is most effective either alone or edged with simple, white flowers. The soft, neutral shade of Dusty Miller is a perfect foil for a bed of wax begonias—and nothing else. "When in doubt—don't" is as good advice in mixing many plants as it is when a woman is putting on jewelry. Make a note each year of your various combinations. It will guide you the following spring when you make your purchases. You'll remember which ones received the compliments and pleased you the most.

If you enjoy sitting on the terrace after sundown listening to the fascinating sounds of the country at night, or if you entertain frequently, a "moonlight garden" can be created by planting a bed of white flowers, especially Impatiens or petunias. These glow in the dark as though they were fluorescent. A clump of white nicotiana does double duty, as it also has a heavenly fragrance.

To compile a list of anything is risky business indeed, whether it is of plants or anything else. Somebody's favorite is bound to be left out. You think this is a cop-out for the chart at the end of this chapter. Definitely not! I could have headed the chart "List of 'Alleged' Best Annuals," but I resisted. Every effort was made to select those plants that are tried and true friends of the some-times-gardener.

By reading labels carefully, you can choose zinnias or marigolds that grow anywhere from six inches to three feet high. Therefore, it can be understood why space did not permit me to go into detail on the chart as to the varieties available under each annual listed. Everything that you buy or order will be labeled or described. Read carefully to see how tall the plant is at maturity—what color it is—and whether it grows upright or trails.

The fun of gardening with annuals is that you can experiment with different kinds each year without great expense or hard work. Unlike the selection of trees, shrubs and perennials, which represent a substantial investment in time and money, a few flats of annuals each spring come to pennies a plant, and the only time spent is for digging a small hole for each one. You can afford to be creative. As with rearranging the furniture in your living room until you feel every piece is in the best possible spot (for a few years anyway), so you will feel about putting together a bed of annuals. You'll try different combinations until one "clicks," meeting all your requirements. One year I decided to try lantanas (technically a shrub, annual in the North, perennial in the South) in front of the greenhouse. It was such a spectacular success, with the plants growing to gigantic size and blooming without stopping, that I repeat the same arrangement each year. I may tire of it eventually, especially as white flies love lantanas, but it will be a tough act to follow!

Some of the annuals I have listed will be considered perennials or biennials in some parts of the country where the winters are mild, enabling plants to survive into another season. Similarly, if annuals are brought into a greenhouse before the first frost kills them, they will live for years. They have to be cut back severely and fertilized regularly, due to their shallow root systems, but I have had so-called annuals in my part of the country last for five years this way. Perennials and biennials which bloom the first year also can be treated as annuals. The casual weekend gardener should take a relaxed attitude towards all this. So long as a plant blooms for him a short time after he first sets it in the ground, and continues to do so for the whole summer or a good part of it, never mind what it's called by the horticulturists. It suits his purpose, and that's all that really matters.

"Killing with kindness" may have its roots in horticulture. Some plants can take a lot of punishment. We forget that they all originally started life as wildflowers, having progressed to today's cultivated plants after many years of intense cross-breeding and research. We all have favorite stories of how a neglected plant turned out to be the belle of the garden. Mine starts with several pots of caladium tubers in early spring in the greenhouse, meant for a shady spot in the garden later on during the summer. Several months went by, and as I brought all my greenhouse plants outdoors for the summer, I noticed (for the hundredth time) that the caladium pots were as bare as a winter landscape. Not one sign of life showed.

I gave it another month outdoors under a bench, and then, in a fit of righteous anger, emptied the pots in an area near the compost pile where we throw pruned branches, dead plants, you name it. It's just one large refuse pile, hidden behind a hedge of hemlocks. Several weeks later, as I went there to throw something else away, you can guess what I saw. Rising out of that mess were beautiful caladium leaves! What an insult to my tender loving care of them all those months. While telling them off in no uncertain terms, I dug them up and planted them where I had wanted them all along. It was one more of those lessons in humility that one learns constantly in gardening. So relax, won't you? Some people become philosophers after a lifetime of study and reading; you'll be one a lot sooner. Gardening is the shortcut.

ANNUALS

NAME	CULTURE REQUIREMENTS						HEIGHT AND GROWTH HABIT							PERIOD OF BLOOM			COLOR							FRAGRANT
	SUN AVERAGE SOIL	SUN DRY SOIL	SUN MOIST SOIL	SHADE AVERAGE SOIL	SHADE DRY SOIL	SHADE MOIST SOIL	UNDER 1'	1-3'	OVER 3'	STRAIGHT & SKINNY	WIDE & BUSHY	CLIMBING VINES	TRAILING	EARLY SPRING-EARLY SUMMER	ALL SUMMER	LATE SUMMER THRU FALL	WHITE	YELLOW-ORANGE	BLUE-PURPLE	ROSE-PINK	RED	MULTI-COLOR	COLORED FOLIAGE	
Ageratum houstonianum — *Ageratum*	•						•				•				•		•		•	•				
Althaea rosea — *Hollyhock*	•	•							•	•					•		•	•		•	•			
Anagallis linifolia — *Flaxleaf Pimpernel*	•						•				•			•			•				•			
Anchusa capensis — *Summer Forget-Me-Not*	•		•	•		•		•			•				•				•					
Antirrhinum majus — *Snapdragon*	•						•	•	•	•					•		•	•	•	•		•		•
Arctotis grandis — *African Daisy*	•	•					•	•		•					•		•	•						
Begonia semperflorens — *Wax Begonia*	•		•	•		•	•				•				•	•	•			•	•		•	
Bellis perennis — *English Daisy*	•		•	•			•							•	•	•	•			•	•		•	
Browallia speciosa major — *Browallia*	•					•		•					•		•				•					
Calandrinia umbellata — *Rock Purslane*	•	•						•			•		•		•					•				

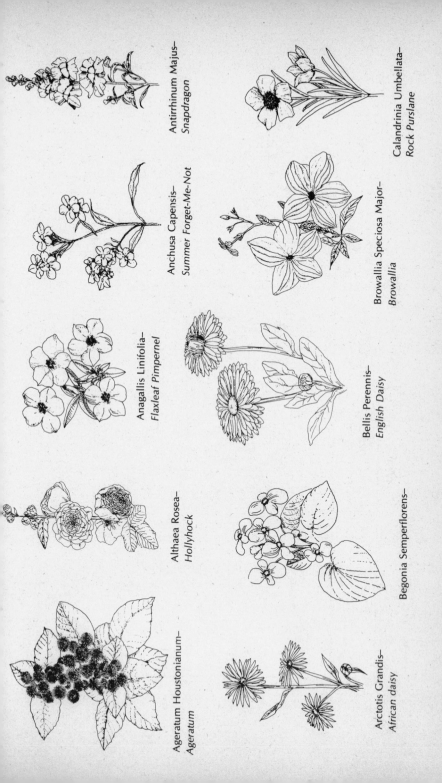

Antirrhinum Majus–
Snapdragon

Calandrinia Umbellata–
Rock Purslane

Anchusa Capensis–
Summer Forget-Me-Not

Browallia Speciosa Major–
Browallia

Anagallis Linifolia–
Flaxleaf Pimpernel

Bellis Perennis–
English Daisy

Althaea Rosea–
Hollyhock

Begonia Semperflorens–

Ageratum Houstonianum–
Ageratum

Arctotis Grandis–
African daisy

ANNUALS (cont.)

NAME	SUN AVERAGE SOIL	SUN DRY SOIL	SUN MOIST SOIL	SHADE AVERAGE SOIL	SHADE DRY SOIL	SHADE MOIST SOIL	UNDER 1'	1-3'	OVER 3'	STRAIGHT & SKINNY	WIDE & BUSHY	CLIMBING VINES	TRAILING	EARLY SPRING-EARLY SUMMER	ALL SUMMER	LATE SUMMER THRU FALL	WHITE	YELLOW-ORANGE	BLUE-PURPLE	ROSE-PINK	RED	MULTI-COLOR	COLORED FOLIAGE	FRAGRANT
Calendula officinalis — *Calendula*	•							•			•				•	•	•	•						
Callistephus chinensis — *China Aster*				•			•	•	•	•					•	•	•	•	•	•	•			
Calonyction aculeatum — *Moonflower*	•								•			•			•		•							•
Campanula medium — *Canterbury Bells*	•										•	•		•			•							•
Celosia argentea cristata — *Cockscomb*	•	•					•	•							•	•				•	•			
Celosia argentea plumosa — *Feather Cockscomb*	•	•					•	•	•						•	•				•	•			
Centaurea cyanus — *Cornflower*	•	•					•	•		•				•	•		•	•	•	•	•			
Chrysanthemum carinatum — *Annual Chrysanthemum*	•							•		•					•	•	•	•	•	•	•			
Coleus blumei — *Coleus*	•	•					•	•							•	•							•	
Cosmos bipinnatus — *Cosmos*	•	•			•			•	•						•	•	•			•	•			

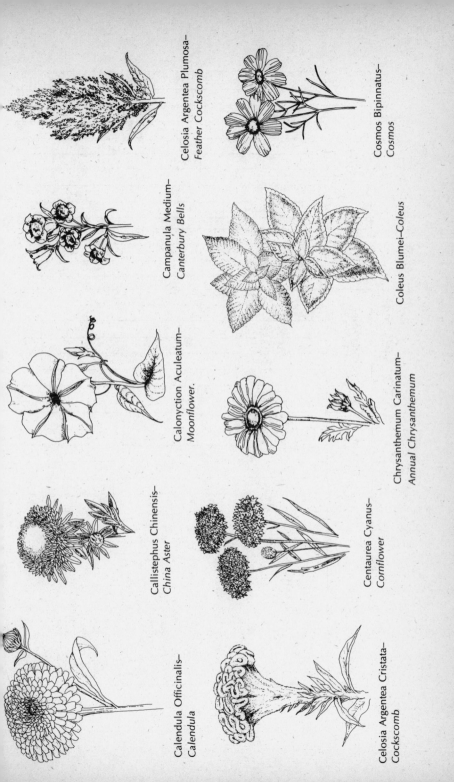

Calendula Officinalis–
Calendula

Callistephus Chinensis–
China Aster

Calonyction Aculeatum–
Moonflower.

Campanula Medium–
Canterbury Bells

Celosia Argentea Plumosa–
Feather Cockscomb

Celosia Argentea Cristata–
Cockscomb

Centaurea Cyanus–
Cornflower

Chrysanthemum Carinatum–
Annual Chrysanthemum

Coleus Blumei–Coleus

Cosmos Bipinnatus–
Cosmos

ANNUALS (cont.)

NAME	CULTURE REQUIREMENTS						HEIGHT AND GROWTH HABIT							PERIOD OF BLOOM			COLOR							FRAGRANT
	SUN AVERAGE SOIL	SUN DRY SOIL	SUN MOIST SOIL	SHADE AVERAGE SOIL	SHADE DRY SOIL	SHADE MOIST SOIL	UNDER 1'	1-3'	OVER 3'	STRAIGHT & SKINNY	WIDE & BUSHY	CLIMBING VINES	TRAILING	EARLY SPRING-EARLY SUMMER	ALL SUMMER	LATE SUMMER THRU FALL	WHITE	YELLOW-ORANGE	BLUE-PURPLE	ROSE-PINK	RED	MULTI-COLOR	COLORED FOLIAGE	
Dahlia hybrida *Dahlia*		•			•		•	•	•	•					•				•			•		
Delphinium consolida ambigua *Larkspur*				•				•	•	•					•			•	•	•				
Dianthus chinensis *China Pink*	•						•			•					•		•			•	•	•		
Fuchsia hybrida procumbens *Hanging Fuchsia*	•					•		•			•		•		•		•				•	•		
Heliotropium peruvianum *Common Heliotrope*	•							•		•					•	•	•		•					•
Impatiens wallerana *Impatiens*				•		•	•	•			•			•	•	•	•	•	•	•	•	•		
Ipomoea purpurea *Morning Glory*	•								•	•		•			•		•		•	•	•	•		
Lantana camara *Common Lantana*	•	•						•			•				•	•	•	•		•	•	•		
Lathyrus odoratus *Sweet Pea*	•		•				•	•	•	•					•		•	•	•	•	•	•		•
Lobularia maritima *Sweet Alyssum*	•						•				•		•		•	•	•	•		•				•

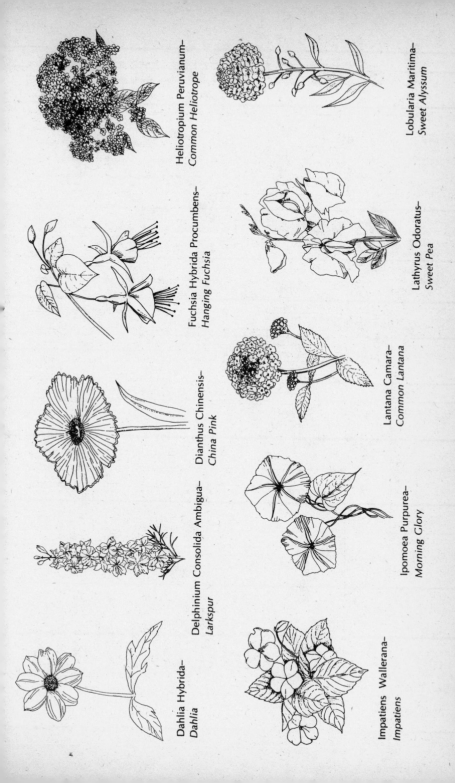

Heliotropium Peruvianum—
Common Heliotrope

Lobularia Maritima—
Sweet Alyssum

Fuchsia Hybrida Procumbens—
Hanging Fuchsia

Lathyrus Odoratus—
Sweet Pea

Dianthus Chinensis—
China Pink

Lantana Camara—
Common Lantana

Delphinium Consolida Ambigua—
Larkspur

Ipomoea Purpurea—
Morning Glory

Dahlia Hybrida—
Dahlia

Impatiens Wallerana—
Impatiens

ANNUALS (cont.)

NAME	CULTURE REQUIREMENTS — SUN AVERAGE SOIL	SUN DRY SOIL	SUN MOIST SOIL	SHADE AVERAGE SOIL	SHADE DRY SOIL	SHADE MOIST SOIL	HEIGHT — UNDER 1'	1-3'	OVER 3'	STRAIGHT & SKINNY	WIDE & BUSHY	CLIMBING VINES	TRAILING	PERIOD — EARLY SPRING-EARLY SUMMER	ALL SUMMER	LATE SUMMER THRU FALL	COLOR — WHITE	YELLOW-ORANGE	BLUE-PURPLE	ROSE-PINK	RED	MULTI-COLOR	COLORED FOLIAGE	FRAGRANT
Mathiola incana annua — Common Stock	•		•					•		•					•	•	•	•	•	•	•			
Nicotiana alata grandiflora — Flowering Tobacco	•	•		•				•		•					•	•	•	•		•	•			•
Pelargonium hortorum — Common Geranium	•			•				•			•				•	•	•			•	•	•		
Petunia hybrida — Petunia	•			•	•		•	•			•		•		•	•	•	•	•	•	•	•		•
Phlox drummondii — Annual Phlox	•	•					•	•							•	•	•	•	•	•	•	•		
Salvia splendens — Scarlet Sage	•			•				•		•					•	•			•	•	•	•		
Tagetes — Marigold (African-French Hybrid)	•							•			•				•	•		•			•			
Verbena hortensis — Garden Verbena	•						•	•			•		•		•	•	•		•	•	•	•		•
Viola wittrockiana — Pansy	•		•	•			•				•			•			•	•	•	•	•	•		•
Zinnia elegans — Zinnia	•						•	•			•					•	•	•		•	•	•		•

Zinnia Elegans–Zinnia

Phlox Drummondii–
Annual Phlox

Viola Wittrockiana–Pansy

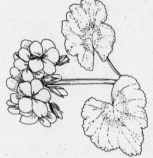

Petunia Hybrida–Petunia

Pelargonium Hortorum–
Common Geranium

Verbena Hortensis–
Garden Verbena

Nicotiana Alata Grandiflora–
Flowering Tobacco

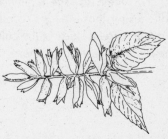

Tagetes–Marigold
(African-French Hybrid)

Mathiola Incana Annua–
Common Stock

Salvia Splendens–
Scarlet Sage

5

How Permanent Are Perennials, or Is a Long-lasting Relationship for You?

This chapter took all of my courage and plenty of audacity, not to mention agonizing research. I can already hear the screams of outraged indignation: "You left out xyz when it's the best perennial in my garden!" "Are you crazy or just stupid . . . you ignored some of the all-time favorites, not to mention roses, of all things!" Let me say right now that it would have been a breeze for me to choose the twenty-five best known and loved perennials and let it go at that. It would then have been up to the reader, a year or two later, to face reality and wish me off to Siberia, digging ditches for those bulbs I recommended.

After careful study of the culture requirements of several hundred perennials, I selected those listed at the end of this chapter by constantly keeping in mind the reluctant part-time gardener I was writing for. No matter how magnificent the plant, I ruthlessly crossed it off the list if it (1) had to be divided within three years in order to keep it blooming and healthy (you'd be surprised at how many that knocked off); (2) had to be staked to keep flowers or stems from breaking; (3) had a very brief period of bloom, one week or so, and then reverted to a blah-looking plant for the rest of the summer; (4) needed to have its faded flowers and/or seed pods cut off or else makes all kinds of trouble; (5) were so fragile in the disease or insect department that a regular spray program throughout the summer was necessary for good results.

I realize that there is no such thing as the perfect plant. All require care of one sort or another if they are to do their best for us, but there is no denying that some are far hardier than others, managing very well by themselves without extra fussing from us. Once the plants are in the ground, the gardener should relax for a few years and enjoy the fruits of his labor. He needs to select just a few from the list, but if he chooses wisely as to sequence of bloom, colors, growth habit and general culture requirements, he can expect a carefree and attractive perennial garden. Add colorful annuals here and there as fillers, and he can throw out his chest with pride.

A perennial is any plant that lasts through at least three seasons' growth. If it lasts only two years, it's called a biennial; if only one year, it's an annual. Most perennials, however, last for many years. It should be noted here that some behave as annuals or biennials if planted in areas totally unsuited for them—such as a native of Georgia planted in Maine. A few, like the peony, outlast the gardener who plants them, and that goes even if he's only a toddler! Almost all require a good, well-drained soil. (By now, you're saying what doesn't, showing you're catching on fast to this gardening game.) But even when this is not feasible, there are perennials that will thrive in moist, damp soil—near ponds, streams, swamps. Relax, I have listed a few of those, as well as a separate chapter. (See "Water Gardening.")

Since perennials stay in the same spot for a long time, they appreciate a yearly dose of fertilizer to keep them strong and thriving. While most plants do well in average soil (neutral), some prefer an acid soil while others require an alkaline one. Don't try to mix them up. It's tricky, and only for the experienced gardener who can keep checking the soil for the proper pH for each plant, adding the corrective ingredient around the base. It's far better to select plants to match your soil. The ideal philosophy to adopt in any phase of gardening is that of working *with* nature, not against her.

For a fertilizer, any good all-purpose commercial brand will do. Bonemeal is excellent, especially for bulbs and alkali-loving plants. Rake it into the soil around the base of the plant, being careful not to get any on the foliage, and water deeply. Early spring is the best time to do this, when plants are in bud. Read the directions on the package carefully, and don't think that twice the amount is automatically twice as good—what if you had done that with medicine you've taken? You might not be around today to read this! Anyway, why make more work for yourself?

As with *any* planting, taking the time to prepare the soil will yield long-lasting, rewarding results. It's the same principle as in painting a house: repairing and preparing the wall for the paint take time, but the paint will last longer and look better. If the area to be planted is well-spaded and checked for good drainage, you won't have to touch it again. Work in some peat moss and a bit of well-rotted manure—which you won't be able to obtain, but since everybody will tell you about it I thought I'd just slip it in. Buy dehydrated cow manure instead and forget dealing with the farmer to get his by-product. Leafmold—which is just another word for rotted leaves—is also very good. To check for drainage, take a bucketful of water and pour it over the soil. See how long it takes to penetrate. If the water just sits there and looks as though it's not about to disappear in the next eight hours, then dig the soil two feet (that's right, twenty-four inches) deep and add a three or four-inch layer of coarse pebbles or small stones. Put the soil back on top. I won't kid you and say it's easy. Do it only if it's a very small area;

otherwise, rent a rotary tiller for one day. Better still, pick another spot in your garden.

Annuals are mostly shallow-rooted and don't require all this fuss and bother, but perennials are there to stay, and they send deep roots into the soil. It stands to reason, therefore, that they get nourishment from their roots—via soil—and the better the soil, the better the plant. Considering everything that has to be done to get these plants off to a good start, maybe now it will be understood why I feel so strongly about no more work having to be done once the plants are in the ground. At the risk of reopening the wounds, let me say that I have nothing against tulips, or roses, or chrysanthemums. They are among the finest of the plant world, and no garden hobbyist should be without them, but—tulips have to be planted brand-new each year to get that spectacular splash of color (they die down or keep getting smaller, otherwise); roses are fabulous, but so is the constant care required to keep them that way. Even the hardy climbing rose, unless sprayed at regular intervals, loses all its leaves to black spot disease and you are left—as I was—looking at bare branches all summer. Chrysanthemums have to be dug up every year, divided and replanted. As with tulips, you could buy new plants each year, but you still have to dig out the old ones, right? And then you plant the new batch.

As with annuals, I strongly advise the weekend gardener not to attempt growing perennials from seed. It's time-saving and far more rewarding to buy healthy, growing plants from a good nursery, either locally or by mail. Not all perennials are easy to come by and you may have to do a bit of shopping around (some of the better-known nurseries are listed at the end of this book), but take heart in the fact that you'll only have to do this once every five to ten years, depending on the plant—even longer than that for some. Doesn't everyone know somebody who points to a plant in his garden and says his grandmother, bless her soul, planted it?

Starting with sturdy young plants places the odds in your favor that they will survive the first winter, if you've mulched them early to prevent the roots from being heaved out of the ground during those late-winter, early-spring thaws. After that, they're on their own. It's a good idea to water them well during the first summer, but use your judgment thereafter. Obviously, during a severe drought they'll need watering, but so will everything else in your garden. Another good reason for starting with growing plants is a psychological one: the beginner lacks the patience of the experienced gardener. He wants results as quickly as possible, and everything in his garden should flower the first year, as far as he is concerned! He loses interest and becomes easily discouraged if he's told to wait a year or two before the plant becomes established and is covered with blooms. A tiny seed does not make for instant gratification.

Putting a three-inch mulch on the flower bed not only will help retain moisture in the soil and keep it cool in the summer, but will prevent weeds from growing. It's also very attractive, as it unifies the flower bed by "tying" the plants together. Keep it on all year, adding to it every so often as it thins down. Many kinds are available, such as pine bark or redwood chips (see the special chapter on this subject) and, as costs vary in different parts of the country because of availability and transport, choose the one that is the most prevalent in your area. This type of "show" mulch is not to be confused with "winter" mulch, which is solely for protection against the alternate freezing and thawing of late winter and early spring. For that, salt hay or leaves can be used around the base, but be careful not to cover the crowns or tops of the plants. It should be applied *after* the ground is frozen since, contrary to popular belief, the mulch is not used as a heating pad to keep the plant warm and cozy during the cold weather!

You will save yourself time and irritation by first planting your perennial bed on paper. You'll have a real mess on your hands if you rush out to buy plants and stick them in the ground. You won't know until it's too late that the tall ones are in front of the short ones and that the bushy types are spreading around the skinny plants like boa constrictors and all the white-flowered varieties are

70

together in one corner. Just take a sheet of graph paper and draw the outline of your flower bed. If your math is anything like mine, make each square equal one square foot. Then make a list of the perennials you want, jotting down their heights, growth habits and colors. Plant at least three of each, but the growth habit must be considered—three wide, bushy plants will make a nice showing, but obviously three skinny ones won't. Allow approximately four square feet for each tall plant (those over three feet), three square feet for medium ones (one to three feet), and one to two square feet for the edging plants (under one foot). Again, let growth habit be the deciding factor. Zig-zag your plants a bit so that you get a "drift" effect, totally natural, instead of neat rows resembling soldiers at drill. Select only one kind of plant to edge the border. This "ties" in the flower bed.

Sketch in your plants and play around with design. This is where your creativity comes in! You are the artist and the flower bed your canvas. Pick it up from there. You'll make mistakes, but you'll spot them—on *paper*. When you're ready to purchase your plants and stick them in the ground, you'll know what you're doing and why. No digging them up a year later in a desperate attempt to rearrange a sprawling mess. The type of soil that you have and whether it's in sun or partial shade limit your selection, but as the chart indicates, enough types are available to handle most situations. And don't overlook the fact that some thoughtful plants do well in both shade and sun!

The reason for allowing so much room for each plant is the same one that makes mothers buy everything one size too large for their young children. They grow and grow before your very eyes. At first you may deplore the "empty holes." Fill these in temporarily with annuals. While planning all this on paper will not guarantee absolute perfection (what does?), it will be an invaluable help. Seasoned gardeners do it; so do landscape designers and architects. And believe me, they make mistakes too! Nature has a way of getting in the last word. Just make a joke of it to your friends: "That crazy plant over there didn't know it was supposed to stop growing after two feet—it thinks of itself as the giraffe of the plant world!"

There are two types of perennial flower beds to consider before you start to sketch yours in. One is a "border," the other an "island." The border needs a natural background to set it off. This can be a fence, an evergreen hedge or thick shrubs. The tallest plants are placed in the rear, the medium ones next (with a little zig-zagging as mentioned), and the low-growing plants form the edging in front. Plant those with white flowers between different colors to accent them and prevent possible strong color clashes. Don't select too many different types of plants, but rather buy several of each kind. This will create drifts of color and design, adding boldness and drama to the overall picture. Perennial flowers are not usually as vibrant in color as annuals, and require mass grouping for effect. Again, use judgment. A dozen daylilies can make a fantastic showing, a flower bed all by themselves. There's no shyness there!

The "island" design is gaining popularity. Perhaps one reason for this is that it presents little drainage problem, since it is usually "cut out" of the lawn—which naturally isn't supposed to have this difficulty. The island can be round, rectangular or oval. The tallest plants are placed in the center with the medium ones around them, and the low-growing varieties form the edge of the bed. Unlike a border set against some kind of background, which can be viewed from only three directions, one walks all around the island-type design. The plants can be seen from any angle. But whichever plan you use, don't make the bed any deeper than you can reach from one side. You don't want to walk all over the other plants or perform gymnastics every time you wish to cut flowers from the taller ones or put fertilizer or mulch around the base.

Should you feel particularly ambitious one weekend, you could cut back the stalks of perennials that have finished blooming, and maybe get a second crop of flowers after a few weeks. Anyway, it's easier to cultivate two small, narrow beds than one that is extra long and twelve feet deep. Don't fall for those fabulous photographs of giant perennial beds. If you investigate, you'll find that they fit into three categories: botanical gardens, large estates and the dedicated hobbyists. The first two have experienced, professional gardeners working for them. As for our hobbyist, gardening is his way of life, and the time spent doing it stands still. Let us admire such artistry and be grateful that it is being kept alive, the way one feels after a memorable dinner at a four-star French restaurant. But there's nothing wrong with the juicy, simple sirloin steak you cook for yourself the following day, is there?

Let's talk about bulbs for a minute. We'll skip the so-called "summer" ones like dahlias and gladioli. They must be dug up each season, carefully stored at correct temperatures, and planted anew the following year. The "hardy" bulbs are the ones for us—but not all of them. Tulips, as noted, have to be bought new each year. It's not so much the money as it is all those holes that have to be dug. I admit that it's a spectacular sight to observe a mass of tulips sparkling in the clear spring sunshine. What brings me back to reality is thinking of the person who had to do the digging—one hole for each bulb. Take it from there. If all you want is a dozen or so tulips clustered in a corner of the garden, then you may find it worth the effort. My feeling is that I want more than one season's showing—a lot more—for doing that kind of work.

No doubt the traumatic experience I had the first year we bought our weekend house is partially responsible for my attitude. In a burst of ignorant enthusiasm, and visualizing drifts upon drifts of bulbs in full bloom swaying in the breeze, I ordered one thousand bulbs (that's right—I went berserk). It took me weeks to do the planting, and I thought my back would be permanently bent. Needless to say, long before I reached the thousand mark, I gave up digging individual holes and began digging trenches, throwing bulbs in like birdseed—all the time looking as if I were auditioning for The Hunchback of Notre Dame. Some of the small bulbs seemed hardly bigger than sunflower seeds anyway. The result was disaster.

I did make a note, however, of those bulbs that self-seed and multiply, making the original effort well worthwhile. They are ideal

73

for naturalizing and come in many varieties. Scattering a bit of bonemeal to them every couple of years is one way you can show your gratitude for their faithful performance. These hard workers are Grape Hyacinth (Muscari), Siberian Squill (Scilla Siberica), Scotch Blue Bells or Wood Hyacinths (Scilla Hispanica), Snowdrops (Galanthus) and Glory-of-the-Snow (Chionodoxa). Plant them two to three inches deep, about three inches apart.

Daffodils—or more properly, narcissus—are also very rewarding. There are so many varieties that a list would be endless. You will do best to choose those that thrive in your own particular area, or, if you order by mail, select those that are described as "weatherproof." These are rugged varieties that will take snow and hot sun in their stride. They can be naturalized or used in clumps in flower beds. Plant them six inches deep and space them about five inches apart. Spring and fall flowering crocus can be added to the list; plant these as you would the small bulbs.

One word of caution concerning bulbs: don't cut down the foliage after the flowers have faded. No need to know the details, but if you do trim, you won't have any flowers the next year. That means delaying lawn mowing if you've planted bulbs there, and resisting the impulse to pull out the ugly brown leaves of those in flower beds. In the latter, you can always cover the foliage by planting annuals among the bulbs, closely enough to do a good hiding job. When the leaves finally fall off by themselves, some gardeners put annuals right on top, but frankly that makes me nervous. Should you feel a bit too energetic that day, you just might dig a little too deeply and injure the bulb. Maybe it's silly, but why gamble? Dig a couple of inches anywhere around the bulb and play safe.

Some perennials grow as rapidly as ground covers, such as Sedum and Sempervivum (Hen-and-Chicks). They are checked off on the list as "rapid spread." They are not for formal flower beds, but they are rightly popular because they perform extremely well in certain problem areas that are sunny, dry and rocky. They're great for cracks in dry walls and covering dead tree stumps (Sedum acre does

74

that in a jiffy!), or allowed to take over in areas not fertile enough for grass. In fact, they can be too much of a good thing, so use them wisely where they can be held in check easily.

Let me explain a few things about the perennials chart on pages 78-83. Some plants you will recognize immediately; others you may not have heard of. But each has a distinct beauty and charm, whether it's the foliage, the delightful fragrance, or the delicate flowers. It's a sort of "one-way street" listing: those plants that give the most in return for getting the least from you. That makes them champions in *my* garden any time!

I could have been more specific by adding subdivisions, as under Culture Requirements, for "neutral," "acid" or "alkaline" soil. The chart would then resemble some blueprint smuggled out of M.I.T. and I'd be the first to turn the page and forget it—which I certainly don't want you to do. I do take it for granted that before you tackled any planting, you went around with your little roll of paper and determined hither and yon what your soil is like in areas where you expect to cultivate it. As you already know, you can then either leave it as is and select plants suitable for it, or else you can add the proper corrective ingredient and presto, turn it into something else. As for what the plants themselves like, your local nurseryman will tell you precisely. So will the good mail-order houses via their catalogs and the directions that come with the plants. And if by any chance you have obtained some of your perennials from a friend who has been digging overtime in his garden, then believe me, he will tell you at great length the exact needs of his beloved plants.

Where "shade" is mentioned, it refers to partial shade. This is *not* dense, forest-like shade, where you can expect only a thick carpet of pine needles. You must have a certain amount of sun filtering through during part of the day. Concerning the height of plants, I had to draw the line somewhere. If a plant grows to about thirteen or fourteen inches, I had to put it under "one to three feet." I also had to be ruthless as to periods of bloom. I couldn't subdivide into each month of spring, summer and fall. "Early spring to early summer'' means late March-April-May-June; ''summer'' takes in July and August; ''late summer-fall'' is late August-September-October. It goes without saying that each season starts and ends at different times of the year, depending on the part of the country in which you live. For that matter, it can vary within the same town! Friends of ours living ten minutes away have their spring bulbs flowering from ten days to two weeks ahead of ours every year. Our location is higher, surrounded by woods and obviously in a cold pocket. This chart is a guide, as simple as I could possibly make it, to get you started in the right direction.

Note that some plants are listed fully by genus, species, variety. There is good reason for this. It means that other species or varieties of the same plant family, while just as handsome if not more, may need staking or require special care. All I needed to know was one negative maintenance factor against a plant, and off the list it came! That's what I meant about courage and audacity earlier. For other plants, I have simply noted ''varieties.'' That means you have carte blanche in selecting just about any variety of that plant. You can't go wrong, so let your creative instincts take over.

The ''blooming period'' is a general guide as to when you may expect flowers. Take ''early spring to early summer.'' It does not mean that *all* plants checked off under that heading bloom during the *entire* period indicated. Some may flower only during early spring; others during late spring; still others during early summer. A few may even bloom through the entire period! If you go away every year during July and August, at least you'll be able to select plants which will flower for your enjoyment before and after your absence. People who entertain their friends during the peak of summer—for weather insurance (that's a laugh!)—will concentrate on plants that do their thing during July and August. It's good to remember, however, that gardening is not an exact science. Plants do not respond to orders on when to bloom, computer-fashion. An exceptionally warm or cold spring can send schedules out of orbit.

I've applied the same technique to colors. These I've divided into color "families," for think of how many columns could be required! This will be more than adequate in helping the gardener design a pleasing color scheme for his garden. Generally speaking, whatever goes well with yellow will be happy with orange, and similarly for blues and purples. The "rose-pink" can range anywhere from pale to intense, but it's still the same "family."

For the perfectionist, I suggest looking through some of the better catalogs. In describing the many varieties of one plant, they give exact shades, such as lemon-yellow versus gold-yellow, etc. Frankly, I don't think it matters all that much. Nature doesn't seem to care how she mixes her colors and no mortal has yet come along who can top her for results. Walk in nearby woods, or through a meadow that is still untouched and unspoiled. Observe the countless varieties of colors, shapes, textures, heights—all in harmony, in a carefree, natural manner. Of course, on a much smaller scale, in a tiny garden, everything is intensified. Still, don't hesitate to try unorthodox combinations. Use your eye, your instinct, and a little common sense. If in doubt, play safe, and separate strong colors with white. You'll get an additional bonus. Come evening, these white flowers will glow in the dark, seeming a bit unreal, a little like stationary fireflies.

Perhaps more important than the list of these plants is the omission of others. As with first aid, it is as vital to know what *not* to do as to know what to do. If, after being warned, the weekend gardener still yearns to plant a favorite of his, beloved since childhood, let him! If the interest is there and the motivation strong enough, no amount of extra work will seem too much to him. Many a cook who considers anything other than steaks and chops a gourmet venture that she can't be bothered with will, once a year, spend two days making a super spaghetti sauce from scratch. It's good for the soul—as long as you don't get carried away with it.

PERENNIALS

NAME	CULTURE REQUIREMENTS						HEIGHT AND GROWTH HABIT						PERIOD OF BLOOM			COLOR							FRAGRANT
	SUN AVERAGE SOIL	SUN DRY SOIL	SUN MOIST SOIL	SHADE AVERAGE SOIL	SHADE DRY SOIL	SHADE MOIST SOIL	UNDER 1'	1-3'	OVER 3'	STRAIGHT & SKINNY	WIDE & BUSHY	RAPID SPREAD	EARLY SPRING-EARLY SUMMER	ALL SUMMER	LATE SUMMER THRU FALL	WHITE	YELLOW-ORANGE	BLUE-PURPLE	ROSE-PINK	RED	MULTI-COLOR	COLORED FOLIAGE	
Alyssum Saxatile — *Golden-Tuft, Basket-of-Gold*	•						•				•	•	•				•						
Anchusa Myosotidiflora *(Brunnera Macrophylla) Bugloss*	•						•				•		•					•					
Anemone Japonica — *Windflower, Anemone-Varieties*	•							•	•		•				•	•			•				
Anemone Vitifolia — *Grape-leaf Anemone*	•							•			•				•	•			•				
Artemisia — *Sage Brush-Varieties*	•						•	•			•											•	•
Campanula Carpatica — *C. Alba, Carpathian Bellflower*	•						•	•			•			•	•	•		•					
Dianthus Allwoodii — *Pink-Varieties*		•					•			•									•	•	•		•
Dicentra Eximia — *Fern-leaf Bleeding Heart*				•				•			•			•						•			
Dictamnus — *Gas Plant, Fraxinella-Varieties*	•							•	•		•			•		•							•

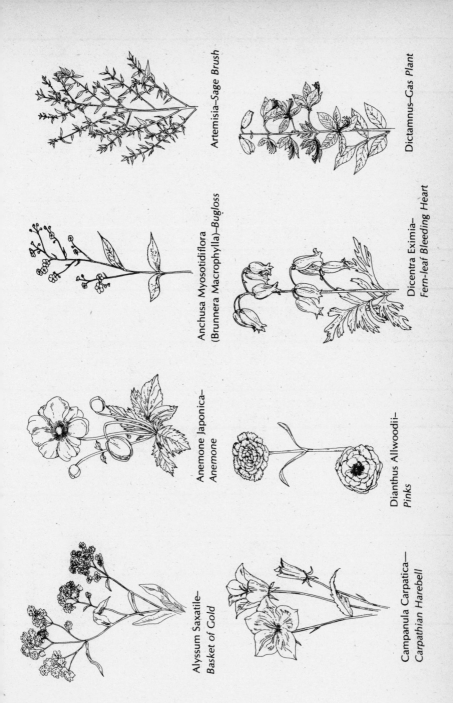

Artemisia–Sage Brush

Dictamnus–Gas Plant

Anchusa Myosotidiflora
(Brunnera Macrophylla)–Bugloss

Dicentra Eximia–
Fern-leaf Bleeding Heart

Anemone Japonica–
Anemone

Dianthus Allwoodii–
Pinks

Alyssum Saxatile—
Basket of Gold

Campanula Carpatica—
Carpathian Harebell

PERENNIALS (cont.)

NAME	CULTURE REQUIREMENTS						HEIGHT AND GROWTH HABIT						PERIOD OF BLOOM			COLOR							FRAGRANT	
	SUN AVERAGE SOIL	SUN DRY SOIL	SUN MOIST SOIL	SHADE AVERAGE SOIL	SHADE DRY SOIL	SHADE MOIST SOIL	UNDER 1'	1-3'	OVER 3'	STRAIGHT & SKINNY	WIDE & BUSHY	RAPID SPREAD	EARLY SPRING-EARLY SUMMER	ALL SUMMER	LATE SUMMER THRU FALL	WHITE	YELLOW-ORANGE	BLUE-PURPLE	ROSE-PINK	RED	MULTI-COLOR	COLORED FOLIAGE		
Ferns / Hardy Varieties			•			•		•	•		•													
Geranium / Crane's-bill-Varieties	•	•					•	•			•	•	•	•	•			•	•					
Gypsophila-Varieties / Chalk Plant, Baby's Breath	•		•					•			•			•	•	•			•					
Hemerocallis / Day Lilies-Varieties	•		•					•	•		•			•	•		•	•	•	•	•			
Hosta / Plantain-Lily-Varieties			•	•		•		•			•				•	•		•				•	•	
Iris Sibirica / Siberian Iris			•					•	•	•			•			•		•		•			•	
Iris Spuria / Beardless Iris			•						•	•							•	•			•			
Myosotis Scorpiaides Semperflorens / Perennial Forget-me-not			•			•	•				•		•	•				•						

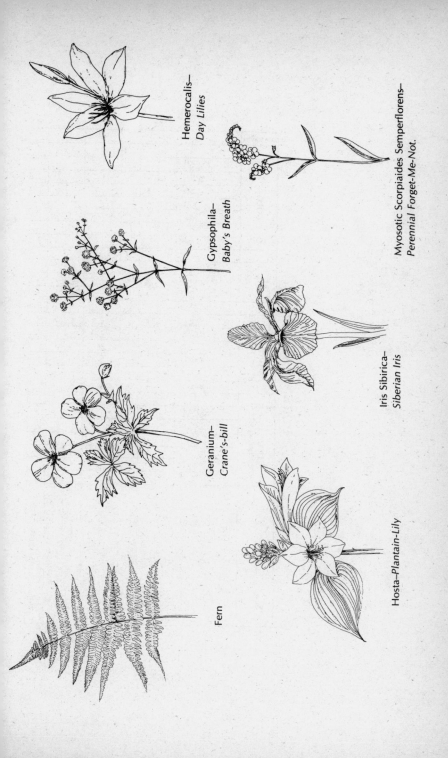

Hemerocalis—
Day Lilies

Myosotic Scorpiaides Semperflorens—
Perennial Forget-Me-Not.

Gypsophila—
Baby's Breath

Iris Sibirica—
Siberian Iris

Geranium—
Crane's-bill

Fern

Hosta—Plantain-Lily

PERENNIALS (cont.)

NAME	Sun Average Soil	Sun Dry Soil	Sun Moist Soil	Shade Average Soil	Shade Dry Soil	Shade Moist Soil	Under 1'	1-3'	Over 3'	Straight & Skinny	Wide & Bushy	Rapid Spread	Early Spring-Early Summer	All Summer	Late Summer Thru Fall	White	Yellow-Orange	Blue-Purple	Rose-Pink	Red	Multi-Color	Colored Foliage	Fragrant
Paeonia Peony-Varieties	•							•			•		•			•	•		•	•			•
Phlox Subulata Moss Pink, Ground Phlox		•					•				•	•	•						•	•			
Platycodon Mariesii Bellflower				•			•							•				•					
Primula Polyantha Polyanthus Primrose						•	•						•			•	•	•	•	•			
Salvia haematodes Bloodvein Sage	•							•			•			•				•					
Sedum Stonecrop-Varieties		•						•			•	•	•	•	•	•	•		•			•	
Sempervivum Hen-and-Chicks-Varieties	•	•					•						•				•		•			•	
Trollius ledebouri Globeflower-Golden Queen			•			•		•			•			•			•						

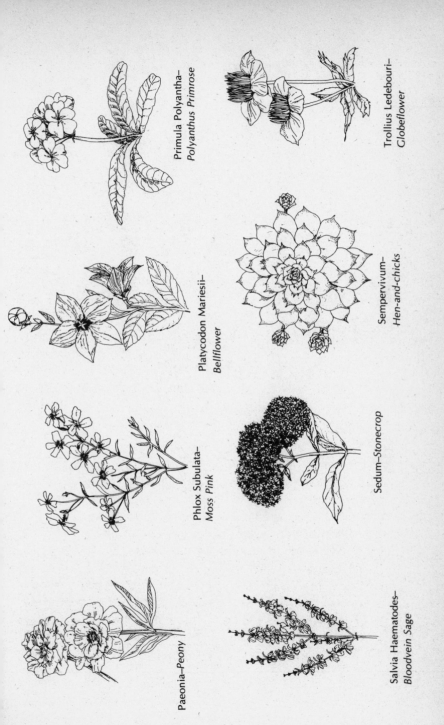

Primula Polyantha–
Polyanthus Primrose

Trollius Ledebouri–
Globeflower

Platycodon Mariesii–
Bellflower

Sempervivum–
Hen-and-chicks

Phlox Subulata–
Moss Pink

Sedum–*Stonecrop*

Paeonia–*Peony*

Salvia Haematodes–
Bloodvein Sage

6

Are You Nuts for Fruits? Vegetables? Better Stick with Herbs!

If I wrote what I really think about weekend gardeners growing fruits and vegetables, the chapter would end right here. Or, in two words, forget it. Chances are that there is a wonderful farm that grows and sells its own fresh produce not too far from where you are located. Let them worry about too much rain, or too little; insects, diseases, spraying, birds, weeding and the many other problems of farming. Wouldn't you look foolish as a weekender getting a subsidy from Washington? I don't scream at my city fruit man any more when he asks two dollars for a tiny box of raspberries. I grow them and believe me when I say that's not overpriced. My passion for raspberries and my husband's fear of bankruptcy forced me to try my hand at growing them. Because I feel there are other lunatics besides myself who cannot live without tasting these scrumptious berries during the summer, I will go into it here. But I can't be selfish. Maybe your secret vice is lettuce. If you must grow something to eat, the least I can do is give a few helpful suggestions.

Vegetables

First things first. Do you have room for a vegetable garden? It should be out of sight of your terrace area and obviously should not compete with your flower beds. Also, it must be in full sun, five or six hours a day. If you have woodchucks, rabbits, dogs or small children, I would advise having the vegetable garden fenced in. You can always grow an attractive vine on the fence to soften the lines and hide what's behind it.

Well-drained soil is important—a deep fine sandy loam or silt loam is best. Most soils can be improved with fertilizers. A 5-10-5 or 5-10-10 fertilizer is a good choice. This means that it contains 5% nitrogen, 10% phosphoric acid and 5% potash in the first, or 5%, 10% and 10% of the same ingredients in the second. "Fillers" form the rest of the percentage, in case you're wondering. Compost, of course, is excellent, as it is on anything. Cultivate the soil as soon as it is dry enough in the spring. This means spading and raking the soil so that it is reasonably smooth, free of stones and debris—in short, made ready for the young plants to be set out. You can tell if the soil is dry enough by scooping up a handful and squeezing it. If it stays in your palm in a tight little ball, it's too wet. It should crumble out of your hand.

Selecting which vegetables to grow is not an easy decision. Common sense may suggest that you grow those which you and your family like to eat. But your taste may run to those that are hard to grow, or are prone to all sorts of ailments, or take lots of room. (Look who has the nerve to write this! But do as I say, not as I do.) A compromise must be sought.

The climate in your part of the country is also a factor. Cool-season crops are grown mainly in the winter in the very warm zones. You should know, based on what you buy locally, what will grow best in your garden.

Beginners (and weekenders perpetually fall in this category even after ten years) have most success with snap beans, peas, tomatoes and corn—the last takes more space, however. Lettuce, carrots and beets are also good choices. And herbs are sensational.

Depending on the size of your vegetable garden, it is best to grow only one or two kinds of crops that will yield a sufficient quantity. You don't want to be counting two carrots for you and two for me come dinnertime. Nothing is more frustrating than to put in all that work and end with barely enough to feed one small child. For this reason, you should first plan your garden on paper. It doesn't have to be elaborate; just list the crops to be grown, the number of rows, the distance between rows, and the planting date for each vegetable. Rows should be east and west or north and south. If they're located on a hillside, run the rows across the slope, not up and down it. This prevents erosion and keeps in moisture. You won't be growing that much, so I won't bother telling you how to group your crops!

Summer to me is salad time. To some lucky people in warmer areas, it's a year-round enjoyment. After all, you can buy excellent canned and frozen vegetables, but not salad greens, to the best of my knowledge. Lettuce and tomatoes can only be enjoyed fresh in a salad. Therefore, they get my vote as *the* vegetable garden—if you must have one.

It's less fuss if you don't stake your tomatoes but simply cover the surrounding area with salt hay. This will prevent the tomatoes from making contact with the soil and rotting. Allow twelve to eighteen inches between rows of lettuce, beets, carrots, radishes and spinach; eighteen to twenty-four inches between beans and peas, and three to five feet between unstaked tomatoes. I suggest that you first start growing leaf lettuce, radishes and tomatoes in two or more varieties so as to have a fairly continuous crop. This should fill your salad bowl! Buy celery at the grocery, as it is harder to grow and requires a steady disease and insect control program.

This brings us to varieties and how to buy your plants. Everyone will tell you that you buy seeds, naturally. That's true if, as already pointed out for annuals and perennials, you are there to see to their daily requirements until fully grown. It is far better to buy transplants from your local nursery. Transplants are small vegetable plants, seedlings, which you have only to put into the ground. Somebody else did all the watching over the seeds for you, did all the thinning out and weeding, and despaired over those that didn't make it. You get sturdy, healthy young plants, as free of disease as modern technology can devise. However, the selection of these plants at your nursery won't compare with that of flowers and shrubs. That should tell you something. Gardeners who don't have the time stick with flowers. Those who do have time, and are around all week, buy seeds. But there should be one good nursery that will have enough transplants to satisfy your craving for "growing something to eat."

While I'm not against using fumigants, pesticides and other forms of insect control in the garden, I do object to any of this on or near anything that eventually ends up in my stomach. This may be neurotic, but it's the way I feel. To prevent weeds from growing between your vegetables, put down black plastic. To keep the plastic in place and make the area more attractive, cover it with a mulch of salt hay, wood shavings or wood chips. Proper spacing of the plants will give air circulation. Keep everything neat and clean to reduce the insect population. If you don't mind using chemicals, by far the easiest and safest is the powder made especially for tomatoes and other vegetables. Simply sprinkle it on; there's no messy measuring of liquid, diluting, spraying, and cleaning of equipment. The powder comes in a handy shake-it can or small bags. It wouldn't make sense for use on large vegetable gardens, but then you're too sensible to have one of those in the first place!

Recommended varieties for your "salad bowl":

Bibb Lettuce: White Boston, Bibb, Purpeana, Sweetheart.
Head Lettuce: Forget it—too hard to grow, and besides, who wants to eat it when the other varieties are so much more flavorful.
Leaf Lettuce: Salad Bowl, Oak Leaf, Slobolt, Grand Rapids, Ruby (red), Black-seeded Simpson.
Radishes: Cherry Belle, Comet, Cavalier, Sparkler, Early Scarlet, Globe, Champion, Red Prince, Icicle (white), Burpee White.
Tomatoes, early crop: Break o'Day, Big Early, Valiant, Pritchard, Moreton Hybrid, Fireball.
Tomatoes, mid-season and late: Marglobe, Big Boy, Rutgers, Longred, Glamour, Manalucie, Beefsteak, Oxheart, Wiltmaster.

A "side dressing" of fertilizer later in the season will give the vegetables a boost. This is nothing more than sprinkling some more of the commercial fertilizer mentioned earlier around the plants (away from the stems), lightly scratching it into the ground, and then watering thoroughly.

Final note: don't be greedy. A few tomatoes will have been tasted by worms or birds or what not before you get your turn. Some of your lettuce greens won't make it or will get nibbled by rabbits (fences are good, but nothing is 100% foolproof). Be prepared to share your crop with these unseen creatures.

Fruits

Are you dreaming of walking up to your fruit trees, reaching up for a juicy peach or crisp apple, and sinking your teeth into it, right then and there? Well, keep on dreaming about it and in the meantime keep on buying fruit.

Fruit trees are subject to attack by many insects and diseases, and you can have a successful crop only by maintaining a regular and extensive preventive spray program. By "regular," I mean every seven to ten days after the flower petals have fallen, until the week before picking fruit. If you spray when the tree is in bloom, you prevent pollination. You should also spray with a dormant oil in early spring just before the leaves come out. You also have to prune. You must select a properly drained site for the trees. The dwarf varieties are by far the best, although they don't produce as much fruit. Now, do you want me to keep going?

You could, of course, just plant a few trees and forget the work, as I do. They look pretty, but don't rush over to them with empty barrels to harvest your crop! Whatever managed to make it past the ailments and pests has been merrily eaten away by birds. I tried covering one cherry tree with special netting; it proved a dismal failure and at sundown scared everyone coming up the driveway, as it looked like some top-heavy ghost. Unfortunately, spraying now and then when the spirit moves you is a waste of time. It's the week-in, week-out program that brings results. Sorry, but you might as well know the facts.

Small fruits such as raspberries, strawberries and blueberries are a great temptation to grow—as I know only too well. And they are costly, with good reason. They require space and maintenance, and the farmer rightfully wants to be paid for these. I learned the hard way. My raspberry patch quickly became a jungle, taking over everything near it—and far away as well. Shoots popped out of the lawn and around rhododendrons, and I had to pull them out by hand (with thick gloves).

Came pruning time, I couldn't tell which canes had borne fruit and which hadn't, so I cut everything down to the ground (only the fruiting ones are supposed to get the ax). No matter how many "early bearing" ones I planted, they all seemed to agree among themselves to ripen at the same time, which was one week before the first frost. Every fall it was a race with time, before the cold "did them in."

And still I stubbornly kept on, saying each year was the last. Then I'd somehow manage to get a good crop, gorge myself with the delicious taste and aroma, and give them another chance.

The only way to control raspberries is to plant them two or three feet apart in any well-drained, ordinary garden soil, keeping the

89

rows six or seven feet apart. Fence the whole thing in with chicken wire at least five feet high. In order for you to get inside this "compound," have at least one entrance and alleys. A square patch with two alleys crossing in the center will do the trick. To prevent weeds from growing in these paths, cover them with black plastic and a mulch on top. Rope each bush of canes to a post (like people being burned at the stake in those old historical movies).

Plant the new canes in the spring, cutting them back to four inches high. Afterwards, try to remember which canes bore fruit and cut *those* down to the ground as soon as you've finished harvesting. The others, which will bear the following year, you leave alone until next spring. At that time, cut them back to about four feet. Remove all weak canes entirely. You don't really have to fertilize raspberries (they're the rabbits of the plant world!) but should yours look a bit sickly, try a nitrogen fertilizer—nitrate of soda or ammonium nitrate, one quarter of a pound to a bush of canes at spring pruning.

When picking raspberries, make sure they are fully ripe or else they won't slip off their tiny stems easily. You need a dainty, delicate touch or you'll squash them before they ever reach your eager lips. Now two dollars a box makes sense when you think of everything that goes into growing this delectable fruit. Even emptying the basket and washing them demand a certain flair. Actually, unless you've used chemicals or you're a germ freak, there's no need to wash them. In their golden era, the French used to wash these aristocrats in champagne. I'll take my raspberries *with* champagne instead.

Some good varieties of raspberries are *Heritage, Taylor, Hilton* and *Citadel*. But do check with your local garden center first as to which ones are best for your own area. That's true of *everything* you plant.

If you have soil anywhere in your garden that is very acid and constantly moist, try a few shrubs of blueberries. If the soil is right, containing lots of organic matter, they'll be easy to grow and easier still to maintain. Remember to "butcher" them every spring after

90

the second or third year. This heavy pruning provides constant rejuvenation of fruit buds. Keep the plants well mulched all year around. They are handsome shrubs, well worth cultivating even if they didn't bear fruit. Plant different varieties for longer harvesting: *Earliblue,* one of the earliest; *Berkeley,* two weeks after Earliblue; then *Coville,* which is a late bearing variety. It's a *must* to throw netting over the bushes once they start bearing fruit, unless you want to spend all your time fighting off birds. You can't win because they'll always get there before you.

Strawberries would appear to be easy to grow, but there are maintenance problems, like starting a new bed from runners every second year if you want constant returns from your work. That's because the average bed of strawberries goes downhill fast after a couple of years—unlike raspberries, which last for many years. There are two ways of planting and growing strawberries: the "hill" method and the "matted row" style. In the hill method, you space the plants eighteen inches apart, in rows three feet apart. Also, you keep cutting the runners from the "mother" plant, and does that keep you running!

In the matted row system, you space the plants one foot apart and you let the runners grow on and on and on. They merge or "mat"—now you understand the name. Of course, there's a catch. You get more and better fruit using the hill system—which is the harder one, natch! The reason is that all those runners, many of them too weak to bear anything, nevertheless eat up all the nutrients in the soil near the "mother" plant.

Strawberries must be mulched properly—two inches of salt hay—and must have the blossoms removed the first spring so that plants will be stronger the following year. Some good varieties of strawberries are: Very Early—*Earlidown, Gala, Redcoat.* Early —*Catskill, Midland.* Midseason—*Empire, Fortune.* Late—*Sparkle.* Very late—*Jerseybelle.* Everbearer (one early and one late crop)—*Ozark Beauty.*

Let me repeat that I have nothing against fruits and vegetables. I live on them when they're in season and you've already read about my hang-up for raspberries. But let's remember that you can do only so much in a few hours each weekend if you want to spend time doing other things.

Herbs

Herbs are in a class by themselves—in more ways than one. They are decorative, fragrant, delicious to eat as seasonings, and, if chosen wisely, they last for many years in the same spot. They are at home anywhere, so use your imagination. Plant them in containers, keep them in pots grouped near a kitchen door, put them directly in the ground forming an attractive pattern all by themselves or as fillers between other plants. The thymes are super as ground covers. Use them in rock gardens, in pockets of dry stone walls. Give them well-drained, ordinary soil and they are happy. Most herbs are natives of hot, dry climates, and prefer sunny locations. Do not add fertilizers, which weaken fragrance, for herbs thrive in airy, dry soil. I am only discussing culinary herbs in this chapter, as opposed to herbs used strictly for landscape or ornamental purposes, and the plant's essential oil which gives it its fragrance is obviously important.

I have selected perennial herbs only. If there is an annual that particularly pleases you, and you feel it worth the effort to plant it anew each spring, then let yourself go, and treat it like the annual flower bed. My one exception is parsley, which is a biennial. I simply couldn't make a list of culinary herbs and leave out this most basic of them all!

Some herbs are like raspberries: they can take over. Where this is the case, I have so noted, and I suggest that you place them where it doesn't matter how far afield they roam, or else plant them in containers. Another trick is to make a "divider" in the ground, sinking metal edging at least a foot into the soil. This will keep the roots from galloping underground.

For those who live where frost is unknown, tender herbs can

be grown without fear of losing them. Unless otherwise noted, the herbs listed below like a dry, sunny, ordinary soil. I won't go into the matter of propagation. Buy good-size plants from your local nursery. When the day comes that a particular herb no longer produces (it can take many years), go out and treat yourself to a new replacement.

Suggested Perennial Culinary Herbs:

Chive (Allium Schoenoprasum) grows to 2 feet. Withstands temperatures to -35 degrees. Moist, moderately rich soil, full sun.

Lemon Balm (Melissa officinalis) grows to 2 feet. Withstands to -20 degrees. Likes partial shade, rich, moist soil. Rampant grower.

Oregano or Wild Marjoram (Origanum vulgare prismaticum) grows to 2 feet. Withstands to -30 degrees.

Parsley (Petroselinum crispum) grows to 10 inches. Biennial. Moist soil, partial sun. Treat as an annual.

Peppermint (Mentha piperita) grows to 3 feet. Withstands to -20 degrees. Prefers shade. Rampant grower.

Rosemary (Rosmarinus officinalis) grows from 2 to 6 feet. Withstands to zero only.

Sage (Salvia officinalis) grows to 3 feet. Withstands to -30 degrees.

Tarragon (Artemisia Dracunculus) grows from 1 to 2 feet. Withstands to -10 degrees.

Thyme (Thymus vulgaris) grows from 6 to 12 inches. Withstands to -20 degrees. Rampant grower.

Winter Savory (Satureia montana) grows to 12 inches. Withstands to 10 degrees.

Note:

A word of caution if you live in an extremely cold climate. In spite of the hardiness of the above-listed herbs, give them a light winter mulch of straw or leaves if your area doesn't get that wonderful "poor man's mulch": snow.

7

Don't Despair –
Call It Rock Gardening

Classic rock gardening is a field unto itself. Gardeners who go in for it are considered the "elite" by horticulturists. Complex books have been written on the subject. Certainly in no other form of gardening are the skills of proportion, balance of space and mass, and sound horticultural practice needed to achieve a perfect, unified design. True rock garden plants are usually unknown to the novice gardener.

The image of the rock gardener, tweezer in hand, laboriously pulling out weeds from between dainty, rare plants, has created a mystique about this type of gardening. Let me state right at the start that this is *not* the type of rock gardening that will be discussed here. Starting a rock garden from scratch, hauling tons of stones via derrick and truck, carefully placing each one after having made detailed designs on paper, and checking for proper grading, right soil and adequate drainage with underground pipes, are *not* for the reluctant weekend gardener. To tell the truth, they're not even for many full-time gardeners. Just leaf through any one of the good books on the subject, and you'll get an inkling of what I mean.

What we are concerned with here is the new weekend homeowner (or any other fellow-sufferer), looking horror-stricken at grounds which to him resemble a moonscape. Boulders and rocks pop out of the ground like dandelions in the spring, and what can he do about it? Some parts of the country seem to have more rocks than soil—I can sure vouch for mine! You name it and I have it, every ten feet or so. Stones, rocks, boulders, ranging from several inches above the ground to one gigantic glacial boulder, as well as flat stones scattered throughout the lawn that are flush with the soil surface. Actually, these are all connected under the grass, part of one large rockbed. It's easy to understand that I embraced rock gardening out of sheer desperation. If you can't lick them, join them—and believe me when I say that it took me precious little time to decide which to do. Such sacrifice has its rewards, for strangely enough, today I bless these rocks and boulders. They give a naturalistic "third dimension" beauty to the grounds, rendering impossible one of my pet landscape dislikes, the "well-manicured" look.

Let us take one problem at a time. You may be faced with only one of them, or all—as we were. Take a stroll around your property and have a good look at the rocks. At first, concern yourself only with those in the immediate vicinity of the house, since that's where you'll spend most of your time. Forget the other areas unless you have a spouse like mine, who gleefully discovered that the *one* thing he enjoyed about gardening was uncovering large rocks. What to do with them once they "surfaced" he, naturally, left up to me to work out.

If part of your lawn area is dotted with rocks that are set fairly closely together, forget grass and use a ground cover instead. You won't be able to use a lawn mower anyway, and you'll go mad hand-clipping around each stone. Where fairly large rocks rise out of the lawn reasonably far apart, plan your lawn as you would normally, but plant a "ring" of ground cover around each rock to avoid that nasty hand-trimming. You can vary the ground covers to avoid monotony, and plant daffodils in some of them for an attractive early spring bit of cheer. A cluster of daffodils rising out of the lush green of pachysandra or myrtle is a welcome sight after winter. Even if the ground cover eventually creeps into the grass, the mower will keep it in check.

If your rocks are flush with the soil anywhere in the lawn, simply let them be. Your mower should be set to cut the grass at least two inches above ground anyway, so it should go over the rocks easily enough. As already mentioned, these flat stones are no doubt part of an underground rockbed and nothing will budge *that!* Be prepared, however, to have your lawn turn brown earlier in the summer than most, since the grass growing on such rockbeds is unable to obtain the needed moisture and nutrients from the shallow soil. Learn to live with this, unless you wish to regrade the area and dump truckloads of topsoil, and then reseed.

Let us next suppose that you have several large boulders, of different sizes and shapes, set fairly closely together. They could be anywhere on your property: at the edge of the lawn, smack in the middle of it, or as you come up the driveway. As they stand now, they are unrelated to one another, looking a bit like a miniature Stonehenge. Rejoice, for this can turn out to be the *pièce de résistance* of your property. You have one tremendous advantage over most rock gardeners at this point: the rocks were put there by Mother Nature, so you can rest assured that they will look natural, viewed from any angle. The greatest challenge for rock gardeners who start from scratch is the proper placement of rocks, for they should look as if they had been there for hundreds of years. It's easy to slip into "studied casualness" and ruin the whole effect.

It's very difficult to describe, but you know it when you see it—it screams "man-made" at first sight.

Since Mother Nature has kindly taken this tricky job off your hands, you have only the decoration to cope with. Fill in the spaces between the rocks with evergreens (junipers are excellent for this, as they come in all sizes and varieties—more about them later). They will "connect" your rocks and set the background for plants. In the crevices of the rocks plant a variety of sedums, saxifrages, sempervivums, or any of the numerous beautiful rock plants available. (See the list at the end of this chapter.) The spreading varieties grow rapidly and choke out weeds—need I add more?

Around and between all plantings, spread pine bark mulch (the finely-ground variety for small plants, the larger nuggets around the junipers). Any other mulch will do as well, but it should be natural-looking, attractive, and blend so effectively with its surroundings that one is almost unaware that it's there. Mulching keeps moisture in the ground and unifies the whole design.

It is possible (I should know!) that you have an area of very ordinary-looking smaller stones, which may or may not be located near larger ones. Who knows, and who really cares, how they got there. Maybe the previous owner filled in a large hole with them, or they're just larger stones that were broken up into smaller pieces with time. In any case, all you know is that you started to remove them and found there was no stopping. It went on and on and you wondered as you kept digging if you would shortly be facing a grinning Chinese face. There's an easier solution: leave it alone. Just plant sedum all around it and let it spread. It will do just that in no time flat and soon you'll wonder where the stones were.

If you have an enormous glacial boulder or giant rock, not only are you extremely fortunate, but chances are that you need do very little to add to its natural beauty. If that hasn't already been done by the wind and birds, which scatter seeds of wildflowers and shrubs, you can plant some choice ones in the crevices of the rock. We have been blessed with such a boulder, well over thirty feet high, and we have left it alone. Children climb it and picnic at the summit. Trees, shrubs, ferns, wildflowers grow out of the crevices. On one side, a tall oak's upper trunk grows against it, so flattened out that it has become part of the boulder. All we did was have the tree's lower branches and those of surrounding trees cut down, to show off this masterpiece of nature.

Another rock, smaller than the boulder, has a laurel growing out of one crack and blooming its head off each year. Ferns grow from another crevice. All I added were Cranesbill (true geraniums which in their dwarf varieties make superb rock plants) and sempervivum. I haven't touched it in years, and best of all, there are no weeds to pull out. That's because these plants spread tightly until they must stop, due to the width of the crevice. It's a miracle to me that the laurel grows at all, let alone so superbly, because I never fertilize or water it (I couldn't begin to get at its roots!). It is a perfect example of plants adapting to a particular situation and defying so-called rules. It should teach us a lesson in humility when we start thinking we know everything about gardening.

If you have one medium-size rock, not important enough in height and width to make a good show by itself, yet too deeply imbedded to be removed, I will concede reluctantly that it might warrant creating an artificial rock garden. Standing there, with no other rock in sight anywhere, too small to be interesting on its own, and too big to be ignored—it's just plain funny-looking and something has to be done. However, keep it simple. Beg, borrow or steal two or three rocks from overstocked neighbors. Neighbors would be my first choice, because chances are the rocks will be of the same kind, color and texture, which is what you want. Otherwise, try a local construction firm or your local park department. Even the town dump. Don't laugh—what you need, someone else may have wanted to get rid of. Place the rocks next to your own lone one, trying to make the whole design as natural as possible. As I've said before, it'll be tough, so take your time. Try different ways of grouping them, letting a week go by for your eye to tell you if it's pleasing or not. Once you've decided, proceed to fill in the gaps with plants appropriate in size and growth habit. Scale is all-important.

Maybe by now you think there couldn't be any other rock problems. Wrong. Do you have a fairly large hollowed stone which collects water every time it rains, attracts mosquitoes, fills with grass clippings from the mower and with leaves in the fall? Since you're not there every day to hose it down and turn it into a delightful birdbath (or you're too lazy), fill it instead with a bit of soil, put in a couple of plants and voilà, a miniature rock garden! In a rock with a hollow, I created a small moss-fern garden, which came about accidentally. While walking through the woods, I noticed how many stones had moss covering them, and here and there growing through the moss would be a small fern. Having nothing to lose (and not stealing as it was on our own property), I peeled off a small section of moss and placed it in the hollow of the rock. I watered it thoroughly for a few weekends, and now it's thriving. It not only "took," but it's growing slowly out of the hollow and inching its way over the rock. The little fern growing out of the moss has remained compact in height, so that the proportion is perfect.

This simple "transplant" gave me a tremendous feeling of satisfaction, because it was done on an impulse and was a total gamble—which paid off. Where there is enough depth, certain ferns can be planted. We are often told that they are hard to grow, but if the proper varieties are purchased from a reliable firm, they will thrive beautifully. Make sure you know the height at maturity, however, as they do not take kindly to transplanting.

Plants which are suitable for rock gardens are usually equally effective on dry stone walls or fences that are built without mortar. If you are lucky enough to have such walls on your property, you can appreciate the skill that went into making them. If such a wall is located near your terrace or in a spot where it is frequently seen (such as facing a swimming pool), you may wish to turn the wall into a rock garden.

This simply means filling in some of the spaces between the stones with soil and putting in rock plants and herbs. Choose some that spread, others that grow upright or that hang in order to have variety in your design. Plant sparingly, however, for as with regular rock gardens, the most pleasing effect is achieved when the full beauty of the stones is allowed to show. The stones are the "stars," and the plants "supporting players." I know that some will disagree violently with that statement. There are rock gardeners who grow rock plants without so much as one rock or pebble in sight. To them, only the plants themselves count. Alpine plant fanciers are among these. Others, especially the Japanese, to whom we owe so much for rock gardening as an art form and for gardening in general, believe that the stones themselves are of such beauty that plants are superfluous. They are classic purists, highly specialized in their own fields. Weekend gardeners are usually only interested in *coping* with existing rocks rather than in *creating* or, worse still, *maintaining* rock gardens deliberately.

To the real "pros," rock gardening is the cultivation of wild plants. Height, form, growth habits are all carefully considered in the proper selection of rock plants. Many wild plants are not easy to buy (*plants* now, not seeds!) and if you have your heart set on a particular one, see the listing of special nurseries at the end of the book. However, don't overlook some very lovely plants which technically are not considered rock plants. For our purpose, a little flexibility is allowed. If you want color in your rock garden and you want to obtain it quickly from the local nursery, there are annuals that will do the job. Purists will cry out in anguish at the mere thought, but remember, we weekenders are a special breed, of which I shall constantly remind you.

My unorthodox definition of a non-rock plant that would be suitable is one that looks at home in a naturalistic setting. It is obvious that formal-looking plants such as roses, ruffled petunias, gladioli and fuchsias are out. Try to visualize them in a wild setting and you'll understand what I mean. Today there are so many dwarf varieties of plants that selecting those that will look "at home" in a rock garden is not difficult. A partial list of suggestions is also included with the other plants at the end of the chapter.

Some basic rules to remember in *our* type of rock gardening:

1. *Proportion.* Select plants whose size at maturity will be compatible with the rocks. Don't smother small rocks with large junipers, and don't plant dwarf conifers next to a giant boulder. Let your eye be the judge. It's the same common sense that tells you that a jumbo handbag on the arm of a petite five-foot woman is as ludicrous as a dainty little one held by her five-foot-eight sister.

2. *Balance.* Again, use your eye and common sense. The aim of this type of gardening is to have the overall design look natural, anything but contrived. Don't attempt symmetrical plantings, which have that man-made label. Space plants casually in groups or clumps for best effect. Study natural rock outcroppings in woodlands and take notes; visit the nearest botanical garden or any of the fine private gardens open to the public. You'll get lots of ideas. Deep crevices in rocks call for different types of plants than do small, narrow cracks. Plants which grow upright have a different function from those that spread. Combine them effectively and you'll avoid monotony of design. And don't be afraid of making mistakes; if what you've planted turns out to be wrong for that spot, simply take it out. It may be perfect somewhere else. Be flexible. That's the whole fun of it.

3. *Selection of plant material.* Stick with plants that grow best in your part of the country. Alpine plants need a different soil and climate than do desert plants. Think of the natural habitat of any wild plant, and let that give you a clue as to how it will fare in your own area. What enthralled you on your trip to Mexico may not only look all wrong in Massachusetts, but will most probably curl up and die. So either buy from your local nursery, or if you are buying from a mail-order firm, describe the type of weather in your locality—with the lowest and the highest temperatures. These people are experts at recommending the right plants and mailing them to you at the proper time of year for planting, frequently with detailed instructions as to culture.

101

One last thought just in case you're still cursing those rocks in your garden. There are people, believe it or not, who *buy* artificial rocks. These look amazingly like the real thing and weigh next to nothing, and are great for indoor gardens and city terraces. And they're pretty expensive! So look again at your own rocks and smile at them.

The list that follows of plant material suitable for rock gardens is much like the proverbial drop of water in the ocean. There are literally hundreds of species and varieties of true rock garden plants —suitable for deserts, cool mountains and all climates in between. Time of bloom obviously depends on spring's arrival in your own particular area. These plants are perennials, although, as with other perennials, they can turn into annuals if planted in an area unsuited to their climate requirements. Unfortunately, space does not permit me to describe each plant as to culture needs, colors, time of bloom, growth habits, etc. However, fear not. You will not be buying blind. You will either purchase these plants from a local nursery, where your own eyes plus the advice of the nurseryman will fully inform you, or you will send for a catalog from one of the mail-order nurseries specializing in these plants. Catalogs, as you will discover if you haven't already, give excellent descriptions of their plants. One good reason, naturally, is that they want you to buy them. But, as they also want your repeat business, they are wise and honest enough to give you accurate data. Some plants grow straight up, others spread horizontally, and still others trail or hang down. Most are dwarf in size (two to six inches high) but some can grow to two feet. So ask questions or read the fine print and you'll be all right. Anyway, I have not chosen "collectors' items" for my list, as these rare plants are difficult to grow and get established, and are delicate and need tender loving care. Instead, I have selected plants which are generally the most popular and most easily obtained.

Perennials

(Bulbs Included)

Bluebells: Campanula (many species and varieties)
Candytuft: Iberis (many species and varieties)
Colchicum–Autumn Crocus-like plant (varieties)
Cranesbill: Geranium (many species and varieties)
Crocus (spring and autumn flowering species)
Dwarf Bleeding Heart: Dicentra eximia (varieties)
Golden Tuft: Alyssum saxatile (varieties)
Grape-hyacinth: Muscari (many species and varieties)
Gypsophila repens (varieties)
Iris cristata (varieties)
Pinks: Dianthus (many species and varieties)
Rock Cress: Arabis alpina (varieties)
Saxifraga–Saxifrage, Rockfoil (many species and varieties)
Sempervivum–Hen-and-Chicks, Houseleek (many species and varieties)
Siberian Squill: Scilla Sibirica
Snowdrop: Galanthus (many species and varieties)
Speedwell: Veronica (many species and varieties)
Stonecrop: Sedum (many species and varieties)
Winter Aconite: Eranthis hyemalis
Yarrow: Achillea ageratifolia (varieties)

Evergreen Shrubs

Barberry: Berberis candidula (under 3 feet)
Cotoneaster: Cotoneaster dammeri (low, prostrate)
Heather: Erica carnea (ground cover)
Junipers: Juniperus
    J. horizontalis douglasi (prostrate, under 6 inches)
    J. sabina (medium low, upright, 2 to 4 feet)
    J. squamata meyeri (6 to 8 feet)
Rhododendron ferrugineum (under 16 inches)
Swiss Mountain Pine: Pinus Mugo mughus (low, prostrate)

Non-Rock Garden Plants
That Look Great Anyway

Diamond Flower: Ionopsidium acaule
Dwarf Impatiens: Impatiens sultani ("Elfin" varieties)
Dwarf Marigold: Tagetes tenuifolia pumila
Dwarf Snapdragon: Antirrhinum Asarina procumbens
Herbs (Kill two birds with one stone because what you snip here and
      there, you can eat as well!)
    English Lavender: Lavandula spica (up to 4 feet) and dwarf variety
      "compacta" (stays well under 1 foot)
    Oregano: Orignaum vulgare (up to 2 feet)
    Rosemary: Rosmarinus officinalis (up to 6 feet) and *Dwarf*
      Rosemary: Rosmarinus officinalis prostratus (up to 2 feet)
    Sage: Salvia officinalis (up to 2 feet)
    Sweet Woodruff: Asperula ordorata (up to 1 foot)
    Thyme: Thymus (many species and varieties. A few good ones:
      Common Thyme, T. vulgaris, 6 to 12 inches high. *Woolly*
      Thyme, T. lanuginosus, ground cover with tiny leaves.
      Mother-of-Thyme, T. serpyllum, in several varieties.)
    The above-listed herbs are all perennials unless your winters dip
      well below zero.
Nicotiana–dwarf varieties
Sanvitalis: Sanvitalia procumbens—trailing

Note:

Most rock garden plants are small in size, "dwarf." This is because
they are usually planted in crevices or cracks in rocks. However,
when you wish to plant between large rocks, your eye will tell
you that taller plants are in order, such as evergreen shrubs. You
can also use some of the same flowering plants listed, but in their
"regular" height instead of their "dwarf" form. So much cross-
breeding and research are being done these days that one can
no longer say "a marigold is a marigold is a marigold. . ." because
one can grow varieties ranging from six inches to thirty-six inches.
Ask your local nurseryman, or read carefully the listing in catalogs

The shady, woodland garden is typical of those near mountain lakes.
A rich variety of shade-loving plants is available for this type of site.

If you're not there to enjoy your house during the summer,
concentrate on a spring-and-fall garden. The spring border of
bulbs above brings cheer to the still-wintry landscape.

Here's a maintenance-free approach to an entrance. This one in the Southwest effectively combines vine, rocks, rock plants and sculpture to dramatize the contemporary lines of the house.

Maintenance-free landscaping for the entrance of a Northern home. A ground cover of pachysandra and stones blends well with the lines of the house. Note how foundation planting is kept low under windows, higher against solid wall. Fence provides privacy from public road.

Locate flower beds where you can enjoy them—near your outdoor
living area. Whether in an informal drift design as in the photograph
above, or confined to a small area as shown at left, they're
where they can be seen.

Lucky enough to have a fabulous vista? Dramatize it by "framing" the view with flowers and shrubs.

Gardening by the sea. An informal drift of annuals provides a riot of color in such a bright location.

Not much is required to bring color to the simplest terrace. A massed border of begonias blooming all summer long does the job nicely in this woodland setting.

Foundation planting requires a good eye. Not too much is needed, and it should blend with the architecture of the house. No maintenance is necessary if plants are chosen carefully. The contemporary at left and the traditional below are examples of good design.

Ground covers not only are maintenance-free, but add beauty to the garden. Visualize the pretty mixture of ground covers above replaced by grass. Not only would there be more work cutting it, but the garden would be deprived of ground texture and much loveliness.

The low, square lines of this house are softened by the lush beauty of clematis vines. Although there are over 300 species of clematis and an even larger number of hybrids, stick with the hardy varieties. It's a rare house or garage that can't be made still handsomer by the use of appropriate vines.

A natural plant hedge or a fence softened by a vine, as above, effectively screens the service area from the terrace.

Shrubs that bloom do double duty. You can eliminate flower beds completely if you select a variety of shrubs that give you flowers throughout spring and summer, and berries in the fall! Azalea, above, is a favorite for spring.

owering trees are real hams! They steal the scene each spring—with od reason. Plant a few for some rave notices.

Evergreen shrubs are hard workers. Depending on size and type, they can provide background for a flower border as at right, screen out a service area, or provide shelter from the wind. Best of all, they're around in the winter when everything else has disappeared! Use them, use them abundantly.

Nothing can replace the grandeur and stateliness of trees. They give so much and require so little of the gardener. Evergreen and flowering shrubs complete the soothing effect of this garden. Except for the grass, it is maintenance-free. Of special note: a mower can go over edge of terrace, cutting lawn right to the edge and eliminating hand-trimming.

For year-round privacy, nothing beats evergreen trees. These white pines define a cozy corner of a garden, effectively hiding neighbors and their chimney. Another two years, and the whole chimney will disappear from view—summer and winter, this property will be sheltered from wind and the outside world.

Old wagon wheels are ready-made beds for herbs. To prevent roots from intermingling, cut strips of metal lawn edging and insert in ground between each kind of herb. Leave peppermint (in background) to roam. This is a tiny herb garden, yet there's enough for the gourmet cook: sage, chives, two kinds of parsley, tarragon, rosemary and thyme, to name a few.

An entire garden can be planted with just herbs! If perennial varieties are chosen, you only have to snip, eat and enjoy. And don't forget, the fragrance is an added bonus to this garden.

Lilies score here! Clumps of day lilies at the edge of a pond and water lilies floating on the surface add color all summer long to this summer cottage and pond.

Phlox and primroses turn this boulder into a tiny garden. It's a
cheerful sight every time one goes up or down the steps to the house,
seen behind the tree.

Far from being a detriment to the landscape, these rocks form a garden
unto themselves. The two dwarf evergreens balance the variety of
creeping rock plants which "unite" the rocks into one design.

arge outcroppings can be softened with rock plants, shrubs and lumps of day lilies.

A dry wall can be turned into a garden if soil and plants are put in pockets! Note that some plants grow upright while others hang; also, enough rocks are left bare to show the natural beauty of a wall made without mortar.

Creeping junipers and pachysandra set off rock and reduce maintenance of path to zero. If grass had been continued here, think of the painstaking hand-trimming around the rock!

A carefree minimum-maintenance terrace, made colorful with
planters and tubs filled with bright annuals.

It's hard to believe nature didn't plant this rock ledge! Ferns, iris
cristata, anemones, azalea, mock lily-of-the-valley, all combine to form
a delightful naturalistic garden. Ivy on the wall of the house gives it
the perfect background.

This is obviously no ordinary house—far from it! But even this elaborate setting is enhanced by the ceramic tubs of flowers (note that they all match). In a heavily wooded area, this could easily be the only flower "bed" needed!

A window box of coleus and vinca variegata, a few pots of geraniums and petunias, and voilà—a colorful spot to rest.

Container plants form a garden in this courtyard and effectively soften the lines of the wall.

(WESTERN WOOD PRODUCTS ASSOCIATION)

It's a cinch to mow this lawn, thanks to the "mowing strip" which lets grass be cut to the very edge, thereby eliminating nasty hand-trimming.

A mower here can go right over steps, cutting everything as it goes along. Notice the excellent design of foundation planting. House is not "choked." Pachysandra at base of shrubs not only sets them off, but provides a "living" mowing strip for cutting grass. No right angles anywhere.

Hanging baskets are the only way to display shade-loving cascading plants such as fuchsias at right. Hang them where they can be admired, at eye level or slightly higher, under trees or under a roof extension. Shelter them from direct sun.

Salt hay is a good year-round mulch for the vegetable garden, or for strawberries as pictured above. Moisture is kept in, weeds are kept out, and you're kept happy.

Selecting colors that are compatible is a must for the perennial border. The lemon yellow of the day lilies is set off beautifully by the blue of the bellflowers. As illustrated here, plant enough of each to make a good show.

By limiting the number of plants, you can make room for a quiet oasis which becomes, in effect, an extra room added to the house.

A lean-to greenhouse can be made architecturally a part of the house—from both the inside and outside. Note roll-up shades and door to outside.

describing growth habit and height. I have had masses of tall, shrub-like Impatiens growing at the base of boulders, looking at ease, in perfect proportion. So differentiate between plants that grow *inside* rocks (meaning in cracks) and those that grow at the base of rocks.

8

Water, Water, Everywhere –
Lucky You

You are lucky, very lucky indeed, if you have water on your property. Whether it's a stream or a pond, it's a whole different world. The charm is not merely the water, but also the plants and the wildlife that go with it.

I am now referring to *natural* water gardening, not artificial. The weekend gardener has enough to tend without building a concrete waterfall or pond. But what if he has a stream meandering through a meadow, or a woodland pond? What if he has a swamp? So little has to be done to add to their beauty. Nature has done 99% of the work. It may only need a bit of thinning out along the banks, introducing a few plants, cutting down brush to make a trail—and there you have your own miniature botanical garden.

Let's first take what you may think is the worst: a swamp. Friends visit you, shake their heads and ask kindly when you plan to drain the whole thing and turn it into a lawn. I know I used to be intimidated at the beginning, and mumble something about doing it when we could afford to, because it would cost a mint to transform that vast wooded swamp into anything. Fortunately, a knowledgeable friend came one day and told me the facts of life. Quite literally, of life. Because that's where it all started, in a swamp. The ecological value of a swamp is so highly prized that, all over the country, aware citizens in communities which have swamps are raising money or putting pressure on local authorities to declare those places conservation areas, to be left untouched for future generations to enjoy. Swamps are paradise for wildlife. Animals there sense the absence of man and the comforting feeling of surroundings left untouched for hundreds or thousands of years.

Other than "cleaning up" a swamp, there is nothing for you to do, except to add a few bog plants here and there along a path. By "cleaning up" I refer to dead trees and diseased branches which should be cut down and made into piles. Unless you have wide paths leading back toward your house and garden areas, you won't be able to take any of these piles of dead wood out. Let them be, as they are often nesting places for birds, water fowl and other animals.

Thinning out dead or weak trees also allows more sunlight to filter through, which results in an increase of wildflowers. I cleared a particular section of my woods one year, and noticed that from two lady's slippers (sometimes called wild orchids, and highly prized), the crop went to six the following spring. Similarly, a great many new laurels were popping out of the ground. It is very hard for the beginner to understand and accept that nature is basically cruel when it comes to survival. Cutting down three young trees to allow one to grow to full maturity is not as simple as it sounds—at least, not until you understand the reasons behind it. Yet, a swamp and the woods which surround it must not only be cleared of dead wood, but thinned out periodically to prevent a lot of spindly trees

107

from taking over. It may make it easier to do if you think of it as a perpetual source of wood for your fireplace.

To walk across your swamp, either to enjoy it or simply to get to the other side of your property, you can build attractive little bridges, as simple or as elaborate as you care. Mine are very primitive. They consist only of redwood planks set on natural fieldstones which are piled one on top of another to form the two "pillars" of the so-called bridge. I wouldn't take somebody on crutches across them, but let's say that they are sturdy enough for any sure-footed human—even one carrying a martini in one hand. If your swamp is fairly large, you won't be able to maintain it, and dead logs will just stay where they fall. They will decompose, returning nourishment to the soil, giving great joy to woodpeckers and other birds. Come spring, you will hear what sounds like millions of birds singing their hearts out, building nests, fighting for "territories," going through their life cycles peacefully, undisturbed. Don't, don't do anything to change this.

Mosquitoes may be a problem, but not quite as bad as you might think. We have visited friends living not ten minutes away, without a swamp and with almost "manicured" grounds, and yet have been just as badly bitten as on our own property. If mosquitoes are bad one year, they're bad everywhere. Spraying around the terrace at sunset will help. Better still, if yours is a heavily wooded area with water very close by, invest in a screened-in patio. It will add an extra room to your house, and let you enjoy the woods and swamps and ponds without the bugs.

A pond, fed naturally by an underground spring or a stream, is another world—an ecology all its own. Frogs, fish, turtles, harmless black water snakes will co-exist happily. However, check with your local authorities as to how "harmless" your snakes may be. I quickly turned to the encyclopedia one day when a neighbor's child (a darling tot) gleefully told me the minute I arrived from the city (I just know he had been bursting with the news all week) that he had spotted a "funny-looking, reddish kind of snake, with sort of stripes down his back." As I have always had a perfect horror

108

of snakes (until I learned about the "good guys"), my hand trembled as I turned to *water* snakes—not those on the *ground* now. I took great delight in reading out loud to him that in our part of the country (the Northeast), no poisonous water snake exists. The only poisonous water snake in America is the water moccasin or "cottonmouth." It's found mostly in Eastern streams south of Virginia. That should calm the fears of all those living in the rest of the country. Black snakes, which we have, live in the water and only occasionally sun themselves on the banks. They keep your property free of water rats, as they thrive on them. They're "good guys," so learn to love them. Well, like them, anyway.

The chief problem with natural ponds is the algae which forms the green scum one sees so frequently. It can be controlled, but only to a degree. Copper sulphate is the best chemical to use, but only with the greatest care if aquatic plants and pondlife are not to be killed. If the pond is small enough and can be reached from all sides, you might simply try an old trick. Take a long, heavy nylon rope, one person holding each end. Start at one side of the pond and slowly walk around the sides until you reach the other end, dragging the rope so that it just skims the surface of the pond. As it does so, it will bring with it the scum which can then be scooped up with a fishnet or one of those scoops used to clean swimming pools.

If this method is impractical, you must resort to copper sulphate. Throw it in, or, if you have a rowboat (here's your excuse to buy one if you don't have one), put the chemical in a cotton bag and drag the copper sulphate crystals several times criss-cross fashion through the scum areas. It is almost impossible to tell you how much to use because it depends on the depth and size of the pond, which in turn determines the number of gallons of water to be treated. If you can figure that, are you good! I've never even tried. If you must know the truth, I just throw in a few fistsfull, and then repeat it a couple of weeks later. I'm so afraid of killing any living thing in the pond (not to mention my water lilies) that I would rather live with a bit of that harmless, though unattractive, scum.

Sometimes, the wind will blow it all to one side, and that's the time to run like mad to your tool shed and get out one of those extra-wide bamboo leaf rakes and pull in as much scum as you can. A heavy rain will clear the area beautifully, but it will come back—might as well face it.

Just for the record, in case you're a whiz at math or someone gave you a calculator for Christmas, here's the recipe for how much copper sulphate to use. One gallon is 231 cubic inches. (If you do nothing else with these figures pull that one out at your next party and watch the reactions!) One ounce of copper sulphate will treat 88,880 gallons of water. Next and last set of figures: a pond twelve feet square and five feet deep will contain 5,385 gallons of water. Take it from there, and good luck to you.

Now that we've solved the scum problem, let's get on to more fun work. Like what to do with the edge of your pond. There's plenty you can do, and do just once. You can watch the result of your labor get better with each passing year. It could be, of course, that you're very happy with the way things are now. You've got some ferns, shrubs, trees and wild grasses growing near the banks, and you're happy with what you see. But what if the pond is fairly close, clearly seen from the house? You may have lawn right up to the edge and nothing else growing there. Several plants that you should consider are listed at the end of the chapter.

I want to stress one thing: keep it natural and simple. A whole clump of hostas is powerful design and dramatic-looking. A weeping willow is delightful with drifts of beardless iris at its feet. Natural stones or rocks lining the edge of the pond will create "pockets" of soil where you can also plant. Unlike man-made ponds or streams, you already will have an abundance of such "pockets." No doubt weeds, at least, are already growing there. Clear some of them out and replace them with a plant of your choice.

Let me reassure you immediately about the best water plant you can put in your pond: the water lily. I was told, as I'm sure you've been, that once you introduce a few into a pond, they'll take over the whole thing in a year or two. I paid no attention (ignorance was bliss then) and went right ahead. I bought half a dozen plants from a top supplier (hardy lilies, not the tropical ones which unfortunately must be taken out and stored every fall if you live in a cool climate). I didn't even plant them with much care! I distinctly remember wondering how on earth I was going to dig a hole *under* water, put in the plant, and then put more soil around it, tapping it firmly. Wouldn't everything simply float away? It seemed like such a crazy, wild idea that I ignored it. I took a shovel, went as close to the water's edge as I could without falling in, stuck the water lily in the mud inside the wedge made by the shovel, pushed it in and covered it as best I could, giving the whole thing a few whacks with the shovel as a final touch.

The results have been just great. I have superb blooms every summer, and the "beds" have grown slowly, but by no means even near to taking over. A six-foot diameter bed took about seven years to grow. I figure it will be another several years before I have to go out in that rowboat and pull out a few plants. Perhaps the answer is to buy fine quality plants, varieties of hybrids. Obviously they do not grow and strangle a pond like something out of a science-fiction movie. I have kept a sharp lookout, and nothing like that has happened. In fact, I unfortunately lost one bed because I used a leaf rake early one spring to pull some debris from the water, and without knowing it raked in the water lilies as well. They hadn't yet "surfaced" and couldn't be seen. It didn't take much to eradicate one whole bed.

I would, however, caution you against the tender, tropical water lilies if you live where water temperature drops below 60 to 70 degrees. They are beautiful and fragrant, but not for the weekend gardener in cooler climates. You would have to treat them as annuals and plant them in tubs which in turn are sunk in the pond, and more which I won't tell you about. (In case you've started wondering too, a thick layer of pebbles on top of the soil in the tub keeps the whole thing from "floating away.") If you live in an area where you can grow these delicate plants on a year-round basis, do so by all means. Otherwise, stick with the hardy varieties. I have found them truly beautiful. They are enormous flowers, some standing erect, several inches from the surface of the water; others appear to float. And you haven't savored water gardening to its ultimate until you've spotted a tiny frog sitting calmly on a water lily leaf, as corny a sight as any you've seen a million times in illustrations.

One more word about water lilies. I shouldn't say this, but I might as well. Water snakes (good guys, remember?) love to curl themselves in and around water lilies, especially if the flowers happen to be around rocks jutting into the pond. They have fun diving and swimming between those large leaves, but disappear the moment they hear you approaching. They really are more afraid of you than you of them. That doesn't happen to be true in my case, but they don't know it! I thought I'd mention this fascinating bit of information because one day you might just be in the mood to reach down and pick a lovely lily to float in your best cut-glass bowl, and seeing a snake slither nearby might cause cardiac arrest. Do what I do: pick up a small stone and throw it in the area where you're going to do your flower picking. If ''it'' didn't disappear before now, it will, but fast.

A natural stream is really much like a pond, only it's long and narrow, and probably has moving water as opposed to the usually calm surface of a pond or small lake. Water lilies are out, but plants that would do well on the banks of any body of water are in. Moisture is the same to a plant, whether it's at the edge of a tiny stream, a pond, or a large swamp. Water is water and the soil is bound to be on the acid side (seashore is something else again).

It's pleasant to have a path which roughly parallels the stream or pond. It allows you to enjoy this extra dimension to your outdoors close up. If there's no path already, it's not hard to make one. Cut down any vegetation that looks ordinary or ''weedy'' to you, leaving intact laurel, rhododendrons and any other native shrubs and good trees. A gently curving in-and-out path will result, sometimes within sight of the water, sometimes not, and sometimes coming right up to it. Place one or two redwood benches along the way so you can sit and relish some peaceful, quiet moments taking in all the sounds, smells and sights of this wonderful wildness. You'll see ducks lazily exploring the area for nesting quarters, returning faithfully each year, and Canada geese circling, diving in for a landing, staying only briefly if the pond is not large enough for their taste—unlike ducks, they're really fussy about the size of your pond! I've tried bribing them with cracked corn—which they've eaten happily, only to take off some time later without so much as a honk, or whatever geese do.

Suggested Plants

Obviously there are many more plants available than those listed here, but this should do for a starter. I have divided them into two practical groups: 1) those that grow right in water which is several inches deep near the edge, and 2) plants which grow in wet or moist areas such as the banks of ponds, streams, or in swampy sections. Swamps which are always under water should be treated as ponds.

1. Hardy Plants for Water:

American Lotus (Nelumbo lutea)–Yellow flowers stand 1 to 2 feet above water.
Arrowhead (Sagittaria sagittifolia)–4 feet high. White flowers. A favorite with water fowl.
Cat-tail (Typha latifolia)–Brown spikes. Rampant grower. 5 feet or higher.
Hardy Water Lilies (Nymphaea)–Red, pink, yellow and white. (Blue is only available in tropical lilies.) No need to pamper hardy lilies. Water freezes solid every winter in New England, and they keep coming back. We ice skate over ours!
Pickerelweed (Pontederia cordata)–Blue flower spikes. 4-foot clumps.
Sweet Flag (Acorus Calamus variegata)–Grasslike. Yellow striped leaves. 2 feet high.

113

2. Hardy Plants for Moist Areas:

Astilbe japonica–all varieties.
Beardless Japanese Iris (Iris kaempferi)–Many varieties.
Bleeding-heart (Dicentra spectabilis).
Cardinal Flower (Lobelia Cardinalis).
Cranberry (Vaccinium macrocarpon)–Great ground cover.
Deergrass or Meadow Beauty (Rhexia virginica).
Ferns–Royal (Osmunda regalis) and *Maidenhair* (Adiantum pedatum) are only two of many excellent species for wet or boggy soil.
Forget-me-not (Myosotis).
Golden Pert or Golden Hedgehyssop (Gratiola aurea).
Iris cristata–Great iris for ground cover.
Jack-in-the-Pulpit (Arisaema triphyllum).
Leopard Lily (Lilium pardalinum)–6 to 8 feet.
Marsh Marigold (Caltha palustris).
Meadow Lily (Lilium canadense).
Plantain-Lily (Hosta)–Many species and varieties.
Primula (Primula Bulleyana)–Also, P. japonica.
Starflower (Trientalis borcalis)–Woodland ground cover.
Swamp Azalea or Swamp Honeysuckle (Azalea viscosa)–White flowers. 6 to 10 feet.
Swamp Laurel (Kalmia polifolia).
Swamp Locust (Gleditsia aquatica).
Trillium (Trillium grandiflorum)–Also, T. erectum and T. undulatum.
Troutlily (Erythronium americanum).
Turk's-cap Lily (Lilium superbum)–5 to 8 feet.

9

Go Lazy–
Container Gardening

Container gardening is not new. It's too much of a good thing not to have been thought of by some bright, lazy, discriminating person. We'll never know who created this form of gardening some 5,000 years ago in Babylon, but we should be grateful to that unknown genius.

Until recently, container gardening was identified with California, Mediterranean countries, and just about any semi-tropical or tropical parts of the world. This is fast changing, however, as it's being adapted to colder sections. And why not? A container is a container anywhere, and it's simply a matter of common sense and judgment as to which plants you put inside one to suit the local climate.

The reasons for the growing popularity of container gardening are many. First, we are no longer "strollers" through our estates, admiring flower beds and shrubs as we leisurely walk along. Our properties are smaller, and we are now reclining-on-the-terrace people. The terrace has become a second living room either during the summer months or year-round, depending on location. We entertain there, we eat, we read, we snooze, we talk, we play card games, we watch TV. The list is endless. To the lady of the house-cum-housekeeper, this is sheer heaven, because cleaning up is virtually unnecessary.

Since so much of our leisure time is spent outdoors, it makes sense to want this area looking as attractive as possible. Just notice what's happened to outdoor furniture. Styles and quality (not to mention prices) rival those for indoor decorating. When sipping a drink on the terrace, who wants to squint to see flowers a hundred yards away? This is where colorful plants in containers, placed with taste and imagination around the terrace, can be very effective.

Second, you get variety, and failures are quickly disposed of. Your friends think you have ten green thumbs because every time they come, your containers are spilling over with masses of blooms, a riot of color. It's olé time, all the time. You are the very personification of The Four Seasons. All those hundreds of prints one has seen of the changes of Mother Nature throughout the year, you are bringing to life! Tulips, daffodils and azaleas in the spring; geraniums, petunias and marigolds in the summer; chrysanthemums in the fall, and dwarf evergreens in the winter, to name but a few. You are a quick-change artist, changing pots of flowers in the containers as your whim dictates. And suppose that one just curls up and dies? Or one doesn't give the effect you had in mind? You know how that would look in a flower bed, don't you? A great big hole, and you standing there gnashing your teeth. But if these vexing situations happen in a container, simply take out the pot and replace it with an "achiever."

Third, it's easy. Containers could literally be your entire garden. Once you have selected the containers best suited to your needs, it's only a matter of mixing the proper soil for the plants, potting

116

them, and inserting them into the containers. If even that is too much for you to do, stick with evergreens. Once planted, they stay put for many years. And you can give your terrace the color it needs by going wild with far-out furniture and zany pillows.

Lastly, in some cases it's the only solution. There are many cottages right on the beach, surrounded by sand and little else besides what nature put there—perhaps beach plum and beach grass. The terrace in this instance is usually a redwood deck overlooking the ocean, with steps leading to the beach. How can you garden? The time, effort and money needed to create the proper conditions under which a traditional garden could exist would be fantastic. You're there to enjoy the sand, the water and the sun. Your redwood deck can be the perfect frame for container plants. Since such a cottage is normally in use only during the summer months, you could concentrate on summer-flowering annuals.

The opposite site also depends almost entirely on container gardening for flowers. I have in mind summer houses deep in the woods, overlooking a lake. Surrounded by mountains, shaded by old pines, these houses are frequently on several levels, with a path going down to the dock by the lake. The rustic beauty of such a place is its natural woodland and wildflowers. Terraces may also be redwood decks, made bright and cheerful by containers filled with shade-loving plants.

Even when the weekend house is located in the country, with every opportunity for flower beds of all sorts, there is still room for container gardening. Once a choice plant is isolated in a handsome container, one suddenly discovers many new aspects of the plant. When viewed from all angles, it takes on a third dimension not generally possible in the typical flower bed. "Standards" are an example.

Now, on to specific containers. One can only be dazzled by what is available. The variety of sizes, colors, styles and materials is endless. Skip those articles and books that tell you how to make your own, unless you're a combination carpenter, metal-sheet worker and mason. These containers will be a permanent invest-

117

ment, so look at them that way. In making your selections, you can let your imagination take over, *with* a few ground rules.

The architecture and setting of your house should dictate the general type of container. If yours is a contemporary house, with sleek, clean lines, an elaborately carved concrete container would be ludicrous. On the terrace of a Newport mansion, it would feel at home, but not otherwise.

Don't buy different kinds, or it'll look like a church bazaar. If you are going to group your plants in one or two corners, buy different sizes of the same style container: one dozen clay pots, or redwood tubs or pale pastel-colored glazed urns. Whatever you choose, it should be simple and blend inconspicuously with anything you may wish to put in it. If you are fortunate enough to come across one or a pair of magnificent containers on one of your antiquing trips, then by all means purchase them. Keep all the other containers subdued and similar, and these will be the *pièces de résistance* of your terrace. They can be giant Japanese porcelain urns, or cast-iron cauldrons or antique wrought-iron planters. So long as they blend with the general decor of your furnishings—or give it that one striking note of contrast needed—you can let go.

If in doubt, or bewildered by the many kinds available, or held back by a modest budget, you can't go wrong with one of two types seen everywhere: clay pots and redwood tubs and boxes. Clay pots improve with age. Their color softens and the "newness" disappears. With or without the matching saucer, they go well with every style of house, kind of plant, and locality. As for redwood, left its natural color, it's great with any contemporary setting; painted white, it blends in with the oldest of New England Traditional.

Clay pots come in all sizes and shapes. The "classic" style is good everywhere, and the rimless one with slightly curved sides is modern and sleek-looking. Redwood also comes in many sizes and shapes. The hexagonal style is more rustic-looking than the square. Really super to hold shrubs and small trees are barrels and kegs. These come already cut down for you, depending on the size you need: full, three-quarter or half. Don't worry about the

118

wood rotting—it will outlast the hoops. Keep the hoops free of rust and they will last longer. Also, don't forget round, white wooden tubs. They have brass-colored hoops and come in several sizes. They too look good anywhere and enhance anything you plant in them.

Don't think only in terms of what sits on the ground, or on a deck fence or on a table. Look up to eye level and admire a hanging basket. Nothing is more show-stopping and luxuriant than a mass of flowers or exotic foliage cascading down a container. Several of these hanging from the lower branches of a medium-size tree facing a terrace can be a dramatic "hanging garden."

In hanging baskets, the plant is definitely the star, and the container the supporting player. Select containers which "disappear" against their background, such as natural redwood when hanging from trees or painted white against a white wall. Clay hanging pots can be whimsical in design, handsome pieces of sculpture unto themselves, so select plant material carefully in this case.

Potting mix is important, because plants in containers have only a small amount of soil from which they must draw their nutrients and moisture. Therefore, that soil must be good stuff, not just a few spadesfull from the garden. Soil in a container dries out much faster than that in the ground, for obvious reasons—there's less of it, and the wind and sun dry it quickly, especially in hanging containers. For this reason, I strongly recommend that weekend gardeners (who can only water perhaps once a week) do not pot directly into the container. Instead, put the plant in a plastic pot (it's non-porous and retains moisture much longer than clay) and set the pot inside the container. Place a bed of pebbles at the bottom of the outside container to help drainage, and then put sphagnum or peat moss all around the sides of the pot, filling the space between the pot and container. Finish the whole thing by placing green sheet moss on the top. No one will guess that it's a pot within a pot. Also, the moss keeps the soil cool and moist. Similarly, with a hanging basket, don't pot the plant directly into it. Put it in a plastic bulb pan first, and place the pan inside the moss-lined hanging basket. Needless to say, trees and shrubs must be planted directly in their containers.

You get a bonus from this method of double potting. If the plant has to be removed from its container, it's much easier simply to lift out the pot than to dig it out of the ground and replace the soil.

Since you presumably do not have hundreds of containers, it's far easier and quicker to buy a few 25- or 50-lb. bags of prepared potting soil. Most of the work is already done for you, and you know it's free of bugs and bacteria. All you have to add to the mix is sand or its equivalent for good drainage, and peat moss for the organic portion. The proportions of loam (soil or potting mix), sand and peat are subject to numerous variations. It's like making beef stew. Every cook has her own recipe.

The "average" mixture is one of two parts loam, one part peat moss and one part sand. It's also good to add a bit of limestone and bonemeal to this mixture. To one bushel, add a five-inch potfull of bonemeal and a four-inch potfull of limestone. Frankly, I'm not all that exact. Like cooking, it's a smidgin of this and that. After I've thoroughly mixed the loam, peat moss and sand together, I then throw in a fistfull each of bonemeal and limestone. I mix a batch which usually fills five three-inch pots at a time.

By sand I mean builder's sand, not the kind you have on beaches. By peat moss I mean the fine (as opposed to coarse) horticultural-grade peat moss. The coarse is good to use as filler inside the containers, as mentioned previously. There are substitutes for sand. I personally prefer perlite and vermiculite, half and half. The perlite alone dries the soil out too fast and vermiculite can make it too soggy, but I've found that the two combined hit a happy medium.

The "average" mixture is good for most plants. However, for those that are strongly acid-loving, such as begonias, azaleas, etc., I mix one part loam, one part peat moss and one part sand. Add the bonemeal, but skip the limestone. For cacti, the recipe goes

120

like this: one part loam, one part sand and a half part small pieces of broken clay (use old bricks or flower pots), plus the bonemeal and limestone.

These three mixtures should see you through most of your planting. There are "recipes" incorporating all kinds of fertilizers that you can add to the mixture as you pot along, but they are not always easy to come by—and if you do find them, they come in bags to last you for the next ten years. It's far better to give your plants a good liquid fertilizer the next time you water them, and every few weeks thereafter. Water first, then give a second "watering" containing the fertilizer. You won't "burn" the roots that way.

Where plants are directly in containers "for good," such as dwarf trees or shrubs, you can give a "transfusion" to the soil by scratching off the surface, one or two inches deep, depending on the size of the tub. Replace with fresh soil mixture and new mulching, and you're set for another year or two. Naturally, these need fertilizing like the others.

I know what you're thinking now. As the plant outgrows its pot, and you keep on transplanting it to larger ones, there comes a time when you can go no further. Quite right. The full-size barrel is just about as large a container as you're likely to obtain, other than those made to order. If you have chosen wisely (by which I mean the proper species and varieties), it should be quite a few years before your shrub or dwarf tree bursts out of its barrel. There's a method called "root pruning" which might help, but it's not easy to do while keeping the plant inside the tub. In fact, it's pretty much of a nightmare doing it outside the tub and then replanting the tree. Only experienced gardeners should attempt this, and without hurting your feelings, I suggest you stick with the yearly renewal of topsoil and mulch plus fertilizing.

In potting any plant, whether in a three-inch pot or a large tub, make sure that you provide adequate drainage before filling the container with soil. I think the best drainage material is old clay pots, broken into pieces (small pieces for small pots, larger ones for tubs). Insure yourself against bugs or disease by putting the broken pieces of clay in a bucket filled with water and household bleach (Clorox is great). This will kill anything that might still be living. Rinse clay pieces well and place them at the bottom of the container, about one to three inches deep (again depending on size of container). Add a layer of *coarse* sphagnum moss (to prevent soil from washing out through the drainage layer), fill with soil, put in the plant, follow with more soil all around, and finally mulch (two inches is average—less for small containers, more for bigger ones). Tap the pot gently to make everything "settle." Finally, water thoroughly until it comes out the bottom.

Proper watering is essential to good plant growth, but so much has been said about it, with dire forebodings, that most people are like first-time mothers of newborn babies with their feeding schedules. I have a very relaxed attitude about the whole thing, and have yet to lose a plant because of it (other reasons, yes—but from watering, no).

You will get to know your plants the way you know your children. (Maybe I should say better!) No two will be exactly the same in their needs. Start by doing what suits most of them: water profusely until it comes out the bottom, then let them dry thoroughly. Test this by sticking your finger several inches into the soil. If it feels moist to the touch, leave the plant alone. If it's like "dust" all the way down to your fingernail, water thoroughly again. You will eventually learn how often this process has to be repeated. So many factors come into play here that no rule of thumb can be given. Temperature, sun, wind, rain, size of container, type of soil mixture, all have a vital role in how often you'll have to water the plant. A pattern will develop, and you'll soon be able to settle down to a routine.

Obviously, if you note that a plant needs watering more than once a week, and you're only able to water it on weekends, you've got a problem. You can hope for rain, but we all know that it rains only *on* weekends! If you followed my suggestion of "double potting," and used a plastic pot as the "inside pot" with moist sphagnum or peat moss between them and mulching on the surface, you'll cut down enormously on the need for watering. Grouping the pots together not only makes for better design and display of blooms, but keeps the plants damper. There are wick arrangements and "bulbs" on the market that also help. The first method involves inserting a wick inside the pot, with the other end in a container of water; the plant draws in what it needs. The second is a clear plastic "bulb" that is inserted into the plant and filled with water. Here, also, the plant takes only what it needs. Let me warn you, however, that neither method is foolproof, but they are helpful.

One last method is also not foolproof, and that is having a neighbor's child come during the week and water the pots for you. Be prepared for him to do so in a scrupulously fair manner: the same amount of water to each pot, regardless of whether it's needed or not. Let's face it, absentee ownership of any sort has its built-in perils, and weekend gardening is no exception. Take heart, however; most plants are killed by overwatering rather than under. Even when they are visibly wilted, you'll be amazed at how quickly they'll perk up when you water them on your arrival.

Comes winter and the first frost—if you live in such a climate—your annuals will die. Empty the pots and clean and store them for the following spring. When it comes to other plants, there are certain steps that you can take to protect them from the bitter winds and cold. Don't forget that they are more likely to freeze than their counterparts in the ground. Move your containers to a sheltered area and wrap the plants with burlap—not too tightly, now. The idea is to keep them protected, not strangle them. You already had a good mulch on, so there's no need to add any more. Strong winds can actually do more damage to your plants than cold weather. Spraying them in early and in late winter with an anti-desiccant (like Wilt-Pruf) will protect them from transpiration (giving off excess water through leaves).

Where you should place your plants depends on the general layout of your outdoor area. Obviously, they should be where you can see them, and where you can water them easily from a hose attached to a faucet on the side of the house. The style of your

123

home will also help to determine how you arrange them. A formal house calls for a more formal arrangement than does a casual cottage. As with the types of containers, the manner in which you display your plants will be guided by your personal taste and your general lifestyle.

There are a few "do's and don't's" which may be helpful. Do group pots together for an impressive mass effect and to keep them from drying out too soon. They're also easier to water. Don't crowd tubs or pots so that branches intermingle; air circulation is vital to good sanitation of plants, preventing disease.

Do remove promptly any plant that looks diseased or is infested with insects.

Don't place any containers on the lawn (unless you don't mind having the grass die under them, and moving them every time you're mowing).

When putting pots in window boxes, put peat moss in the spaces and green sheet moss on the top. This way, you won't be able to tell that they're not growing right out of the window box itself. When one stops blooming or looks sickly, simply lift it out and replace with another.

For woody ornamentals, a simple "5-10-5" fertilizer is good. So is any other complete fertilizer containing nitrogen, phosphorus and potassium. That's what the numbers mean. Never fertilize at planting time; wait a few weeks. Once a month is plenty when it comes to fertilizing any of your containers. Actually, late spring, and then again mid-summer, should suffice.

It's a good idea to stake trees and large shrubs. You never know when strong winds will come along and do real damage. In the case of "standards," make sure that the stake goes all the way up to the "head." It had taken me quite a few years to grow a "standard" fuchsia tree from a small cutting. The stake I used did not reach all the way up, leaving the extra inches at the top on their own. When I arrived in the country one weekend, there was the "head" of my pet tree totally snapped off. All that remained was a tall stick. This sad tale taught me a lesson, but it also has a happy ending. I couldn't bear to throw away the poor thing, so I hid it somewhere in the rear of the garden. After several weeks, I noticed that a few tiny leaves were growing out of the "stick." Within six months, I had a "head" on my tree once more. To tell the truth, it was fuller than the previous one! Talk about the benefits of severe pruning!

You can stake your larger plants without having to sacrifice looks. Buy green wood stakes and attach the plant to the stake with green wire strung through pieces of green garden hose. If you tie in spots that are fairly bushy, you won't notice anything. This is good for shrubs. For single-stem plants or trees, use natural-color wood stakes and beige or brown wire and hose pieces. The idea is to use camouflage techniques, having the staking equipment blend with the plant.

In areas where winters are severe, place straw or salt hay all around the containers to protect the plants against extreme cold.

Keep up regular weekly watering of all your container plants until the soil freezes (year-round if yours is a mild climate). Begin watering again as soon as the soil thaws in the spring, removing any protective material used other than the permanent mulch. If you have no sheltered area in your garden, bring your hardy deciduous and evergreen plants into a garage or cool basement. As these plants will not have their soil freeze—unlike those left outdoors—keep on watering them occasionally.

Almost *anything* can be grown in a container, but here are a few suggestions:

Annuals or Perennials
(All to be treated as annuals)

Ageratum–Sun. Soft violet-blue flowers.
Begonias– So many to choose from! For shade, choose those that are prized for their foliage; for sun, stick to the semperflorens. A bit tricky but spectacular are the hanging tuberous begonias. Place a hanging basket

of these on the branch of a tree (thereby giving it the part shade it needs) and it's quite a sight. Not for dry, hot climates. Likes cool nights and humidity.

Browallia speciosa major—Lots of tiny blue flowers with glossy foliage. Part shade.

Bulbs—Great for containers. Resist temptation to mix them. Daffodils, tulips, grape hyacinths (muscari), fragrant hyacinths are all best planted alone, but crowded for lush effect.

Chrysanthemums (C. morifolium)—Upright or hanging. Sun. Many colors.

English Ivy (Hedera Helix)—Ideal as edging for hanging baskets and mixed in with flowers in window boxes.

Ferns—Beautiful as accent and background for flowering plants. Many species and varieties to choose from

Fuchsias—Hanging varieties are best. Excellent dangling from lower branches of trees, next to cascading tuberous begonias. Like same type of climate.

Geraniums (Pelagornium)—There are now so many beautiful varieties and colors of this faithful, profusely blooming plant, that it can no longer be called the ''commonest'' of container plants. Sun. Upright or trailing (ivy geranium).

Herbs—Almost any herb can be grown. (See Chapter 6 for list.) Those that are likely to ''take over'' in a regular bed are made for containers! Keep these by themselves. Don't mix them with other herbs. Boxes or barrels with wooden partitions are good. As most herbs like soil on the dry side, there's not the same problem as with other plants. However, the method of putting several pots into a larger container works as well with herbs as with other plants.

Impatiens—Avoid fancy hybrids. Shade. For masses of blooms, choose the common variety, in white, orange, pink.

Lantanas—Upright or trailing varieties. Full sun. Vigorous bloomer in many combinations of color (pale purple only in trailing variety).

Lobelia (L. erinus)—Upright or trailing varieties. Part shade. Blooms summer and fall. Soft blue flowers. Variety ''alba'' has white flowers.

Marigolds (Tagetes)—Dwarf varieties best. Sun. Solid or combinations of yellow, orange, red and bronze.

Petunias (P. hybrida)—Choose dwarf varieties or the trailing types for window boxes or to cascade from tall containers. Full sun, except in dry, excessively hot inland areas, where part shade is best. Wide color range.

Sedum—Many species—good for hanging baskets. Full sun.

Succulents—Easy to grow, fun to group different species and varieties in large containers. Require little watering, full sun.

Sweet Alyssum (Lobularia maritima)—Spreading plant; excellent as cascad-

126

ing edging plant to taller, upright ones in middle of container. White or lavender flowers.

Shrubs and Trees

Important: Any planting done above-ground is naturally subject to greater dangers than its counterpart in regular below-ground situations. Both heat and cold are intensified in container gardening; therefore, check carefully with your local nurseryman as to the year-round hardiness of shrubs and trees you select as permanent container plants. As it is, "permanent" in this form of gardening is not the same as with the usual one. But it does mean getting several years, even in cold climates, from a plant, instead of merely one season.

American Arborvitae (Thuja occidentalis)–Hardy evergreen.

Azalea–Many species and varieties, but Belgian Indicas and Jurumes are best. Won't take frost.

Bamboo (Bambusa)–For light, airy effect. Won't take frost.

Boxwood (Buxus)–Hardy evergreen.

Camellia japonica–formal, majestic beauty. Many colors and various heights according to varieties. Won't take frost.

Canadian Hemlock (Tsuga canadensis)–Hardy evergreen. (Also see page 36.)

Citrus–Orange, lemon, lime—pick your favorite, but don't count on harvesting your breakfast food. Won't take frost.

Cornelian Cherry (Cornus mas)–Hardy, deciduous tree.

Crab-Apple (Malus)–Hardy, deciduous tree. (Also see page 35.)

Gardenia–Fabulous fragrance, evergreen luxurious foliage, waxy-white flowers. Won't take frost.

Japanese Andromeda (Pieris japonica)–Handsome evergreen shrub. (Also see page 41.)

Japanese Holly (Ilex crenata)–Handsome hardy evergreen, as are all the hollies!

Juniper (Juniperus)–Hardy evergreen. Will take wind. (Also see page 41.)

Oleander (Nerium oleander)–Evergreen shrub with profuse flowers available in many colors. Won't take frost.

127

Palm, Dwarf (Neantha bella)—There are many, some hardier than others. Graceful plants. Won't take frost.

Pine (Pinus)—Hardy evergreen. Will take wind. (Also see page 36.)

Spruce (Picea)—Hardy evergreen. (Also see page 36.)

Winged Euonymus (Euonumus alatus)—Hardy deciduous shrub. (Also see page 39.)

A repeat word of caution: Containers filled with annuals or perennials should be looked upon as one-season plants. Throw them out with the first frost, and start all over again next spring. Stick with those that "proved" themselves best for your setting, or experiment with a whole new batch. That's the ease and fun of container gardening. When it comes to shrubs and trees, I'll say it again: as this is a far more costly investment, select what is hardy in your area all year around—given some protection, as already discussed. Anything that grows in the ground can grow in a suitable container, but it usually will be much smaller in height and width. Thus, your forest hemlock will not be the same giant in your tub, but it will be a most handsome specimen nonetheless. For this reason, it is best to start out with a dwarf form of a particular plant—if one exists—to save transplanting later or at least to postpone it for a while.

10

If It's Green, Call It a Lawn

It's a fair guess that the lawn is the number-one topic of conversation with male gardeners. Perhaps it's because they're the ones who usually take care of it, even if they do nothing else around the house. Flowers and such stuff are usually "left to the women," especially in this country.

Short of having your own resident greenskeeper, if one even hears the term anymore, a perfect lawn is a nice daydream. If one could eavesdrop on a conversation among the professionals hired by country clubs to keep their golf courses in tip-top shape, particularly the greens, one would shudder and install fence-to-fence outdoor carpeting.

Let's get back to basics. Why does anyone want a lawn? Because it's soothing to the eye to see a stretch of green "tying together" the house, terrace, shrubs and flower beds. It's the unifying *color* green that does the trick. From a distance, this is the magic of a lawn. Not until you come right up to it and stare intently at your feet are you conscious of certain weeds growing in the grass (unless the weeds are blooming, of course—which is sort of pretty, really).

The national obsession with a perfect lawn puts it almost in the status symbol category. Never have so many spent so much time, effort and money on something that yields so little, compared to a fair-to-good lawn teamed with ground covers and shrubs. For the weekend gardener, it would be sheer folly to aspire to a perfect billiard-table lawn. The pros work full-time at it, using the latest chemicals (some of which we're not allowed by law to use) and the newest seeds with which they are constantly experimenting, not to mention daily, deep watering. And they still have problems!

Patience and more patience is really all you need to have a fair-to-good lawn. If every year you faithfully feed your lawn, reseeding bald spots, eventually it will take hold, get a good root system, and thereby choke out the weeds. The regular use of weed-control chemicals rounds out the schedule. Unless absolutely necessary, don't start a lawn from scratch. Try to salvage what you have. The lawn I inherited from the previous owner was a total disaster. To call it a lawn is really not accurate. It was an exotic melange of grasses, with over 50% weeds. A steady program of feeding and weed-control has finally brought it to the point where I no longer blush beet-red when I refer to *it* as the lawn. It's far from perfect and will always have weeds, but when seen from a distance, it *is* a carpet of green. That's all I want and need.

Because of the preoccupation of homeowners with lawns, research never stops and new products keep appearing each spring in garden supply stores. The experts are the first to admit that the perfect seed and the fool-proof chemical have yet to be discovered. For this reason it is best to mix your seeds—two or three Kentucky blues, or two or three fescues. Always check first with your local nursery and read the local newspaper garden section as to the latest products that are best for your part of the country.

Don't try to grow lawn where you know it will never make it. And you'll know, all right. You'll spend a small fortune trying, only to turn finally to ground covers, which you should have done in the first place. Dense shade, rocky areas, inadequate rainfall during growing season, and poor, sandy soil will put all the odds against you.

Let's briefly go over what it takes to make a brand-new lawn. The pH of your soil should be around 6 to 6.5. Bring out your little kit again! This is important because lawns and acid soils do not hit it off. Add limestone to make your soil more alkaline. Eighty pounds of the stuff per thousand square feet should do the trick. Next, to improve the quality of your soil (which should be at least six to eight inches deep), add a half-inch cover of superphosphate and three to four bales of peat moss for every thousand square feet. Rock phosphate or bonemeal can be substituted for the superphosphate, but it will take longer to break down. All of the above ingredients can be put down at the same time, and rototilled thoroughly to a depth of eight to twelve inches. Rent or borrow this hand tilling machine, or you're going to have the sorest muscles in town. Without it, you will have to turn the soil several times with a spading fork to mix the "stew" good and proper.

The next step is to rake the soil so that all stones, debris, roots and such are out of the ground. This should leave you with a smooth surface. No humps or hollows allowed! Now is the time to correct any such blemishes. Use a fumigant, following instructions carefully, to give you a sterile bed. This will kill everything to a depth of four to six inches, so be careful where you use it. Keep away from trees and shrubs. You can seed two weeks afterwards.

Buy the best grass seed available which is made especially for your area. Many garden supply stores have mixtures which are just for their town and the immediate vicinity. Proper selection of seed cannot be overemphasized. Get a variety, since out of it something is bound to grow! Do not pay extra for hormonized seed. Grass seed is not improved by treatment with hormone powders. The rates of seeding for new lawns—the number of pounds of seed for each thousand square feet—depends largely on the type of seed you buy. A guideline: four pounds for Bluegrass mixture; six pounds for Red fescue mixture. Again, read directions on the package carefully.

Sowing seed takes a delicate touch, since you want to spread it evenly and not have bunches of grass with bare spots in between. A mechanical spreader is a handy little thing to have for this, and is very inexpensive. If you go for the idea of looking like The Sower, right out of an old painting, then mix your seeds half and half with sand or fine topsoil to give you more material to work with as you wave your arms about. *Don't* do it on a windy day. Scatter half of the seed in one direction, walking back and forth in parallel lines. Then scatter the other half walking in lines at right angles to the first. Get the idea? You criss-cross your area this way, and the grass won't grow in unnaturally neat rows.

After the seed is sown, rake the soil lightly. Cover the seed only about an eighth of an inch. Unless you stick to this, forget it. Leave it alone rather than lose the seed. Go over the area with a lawn roller to firm the soil about the seeds. Again, you can skip this procedure. It will just take a bit longer for the seeds to germinate. Skip mulching—it will do more harm than good if not handled carefully. Usually there's enough rainfall in autumn (when this should be done) to keep the seeds moist. If there isn't, you'll have to make arrangements with somebody to come during your absence and sprinkle the new seed bed. It should be kept moist but not soaking wet. Obviously, keep pets and children away from the area.

Nature will now take over and you should have a nice new lawn. Mow as soon as the grass is tall enough to reach the mower blades, which should be set for two inches. This is a good height to maintain, as it prevents the lawn from drying out during the hot summer months. Mow often enough (once a week unless you have an awfully rainy summer) to prevent matted clippings from clogging the grass, since you certainly don't want to add raking to the mowing chores!

You can have instant gratification if, after you've followed the exact routine outlined above, you have sod installed. You will be about one year ahead of the seeded lawn this way, and look at the work you've saved yourself. Naturally, it's more expensive, because somebody else had to do the job, but if you have only a small space to cover (smart you), you might find it well worthwhile. But you'll have to prepare the bed just as carefully and keep the sod moist until the roots take hold two or three weeks later.

If you are going to water your lawn, once it is established, do it regularly and deeply. Check to see when the soil *beneath* the turf is dry, and then water until it reaches the roots four to six inches below. How long this will take depends on the type of sprinkler you use and your water pressure. Time it by placing an empty coffee can under the sprinkler. When the water is one inch deep, turn it off. This should be enough to soak the soil to the desired depth of four to six inches. Check to be sure, then stick to this schedule. Once a week is average for this kind of watering, but different types of soil dry out at varying rates.

What about your old lawn? A lot can be done about it. Simply take the following steps.

In early spring, apply a pre-emergent crabgrass killer. Some of these interfere seriously with any seeding made the same season or injure some types of grasses. The safest to date is Siduron (Tupersan). It is safe everywhere on everything. Siduron is the trade name. As with drugs, it is always less expensive to buy products by their generic names whenever available.

In spring feed the lawn with a 100% non-organic 10-6-4 fertilizer (that means 10% nitrogen, 6% phosphoric acid and 4% potash as the chief ingredients). Apply at the rate described on the bag. This is important; too much will burn the turf. Two weeks later, apply a broad-leaf weed killer (2, 4-D or Silvex is good, but be careful near trees and don't pick a windy day). A second fertilizing can

133

be done in early June if desired. Use a slow-release 50% organic fertilizer only, of 10-6-4.

In mid-August, cut the grass a bit shorter and rake out all grass clippings and debris. Use a thatching machine (better get acquainted with the local rental agency) or a steel rake to remove excess thatch. Apply lime if needed (test the soil every few years) and give another dose of fertilizer in early September—100% organic only, of 10-6-4. Loosen the soil in the bare spots and seed. Rake lightly and put on a light coat of topsoil to cover the seed. Water to keep it moist.

The more you fertilize the grass, the better it will grow. It's that simple. If you wish to splurge a bit, in early October you can give a fourth and last fertilizing of 50% organic, 10-6-4. This is drastic medicine for a really sick lawn, but it works. For the average lawn, two feedings are sufficient: one in early spring, and another in early fall.

If you follow this basic procedure faithfully each year, your lawn should improve visibly. Also, if you *know* and can isolate the particular disease or insect that is ravaging the grass, you can buy a specific product to control it. (See the chapter on pesticides.) There is a chemical for every ailment, but unless the damage is noticeable, you'd be pushing that spreader all summer if you went after every bug. A healthy, well-fed lawn will resist disease, so put your money in fertilizers. Inorganic fertilizers are the least expensive but require care in applying during the growing season. Natural organic and slow-acting synthetics (urea-forms) release their nutrients more slowly. They are more expensive, but the danger of burning the turf is reduced. Both are equally effective.

If you have someone coming during the week to mow your lawn (lucky you), have it done late in the week. You'd be surprised how quickly grass can grow at certain times of the year, and if you have it cut on a Monday or Tuesday, by the time you arrive at your weekend retreat the grass will be in need of it again. For your enjoyment and that of your weekend guests, have it done Friday or early Saturday.

134

You are among the fortunate if your lawn area is fairly smooth and level, as well as "all in one piece" as opposed to a free-form design going hither and yon. For Christmas you can invest in an irrigation system. This underground sprinkler arrangement can take over the task of watering and keep your lawn looking green even during the summer months. At a flick of a switch, the water turns on a fine spray to cover the entire area, for the length of time you have set. But it's no good if your lawn is all chopped up or if your water pressure is sad. Unless you can water regularly and deeply, it is best to skip it altogether (happy news!). A mere sprinkling will only invite disease.

Remember what was said at the beginning of this book when you were planning your garden: put in some kind of mowing strip all around the lawn—whether natural like a ground cover, or man-made of bricks or wood or such. The power mower can then straddle the strip to cut the grass down right to the very edge—saving you one of the most annoying of all gardening chores, hand-trimming.

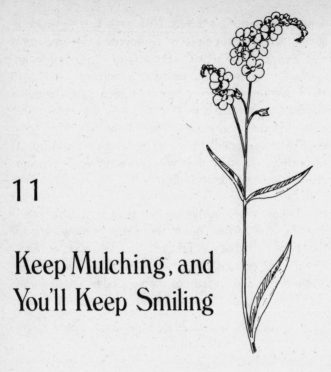

11

Keep Mulching, and You'll Keep Smiling

The beauty of mulching is that while you are doing yourself a great big favor, you are also being good to the plants! I'm for anything that has multiple benefits. Just what is a mulch? Any material applied in depth to cover the ground around planting material. Nature does it her way with leaves, ground cover plants and, of course, snow in the winter.

The reasons for mulching are many. The most important ones for weekend gardeners are (1) preventing weeds so that only a few will have to be pulled out by hand, and (2) conservation of moisture in the soil, which means less watering to be done, if any. Now, when you realize how time-consuming these two chores are, not to mention that they're not exactly exciting, you must admit mulching is in your corner fighting.

A mulched soil also encourages roots of plants to develop in the topsoil, which is the best soil in the garden—like the cream in your milk! Root injury from deep cultivation and hoeing is eliminated, since you don't have to bother with either. A mulch, in breaking down slowly into the soil, adds nutrients as well as making it more friable, thanks to the decaying organic matter. Soil will not become compacted when walked on while still moist from rain, if it is mulched.

Properly applied, a mulch will reduce, by at least half, the amount of water lost from the soil by evaporation. Since plants should go into winter with as much water in their systems as possible, you can see this value immediately. A winter mulch is needed because without a snow cover (and who can guarantee that except in northern regions), plants can be heaved out of the soil by frost action. The late-winter, early-spring thaws can expose surface roots and do great damage.

The way to solve the summer and winter mulching problem is simply to have a year-round mulch. Select an attractive material and keep adding a bit each year or so, maintaining a depth of anywhere from two to six inches, depending on the type that you use. After all, this is the way nature works—it doesn't go around putting leaves on and taking them off. The reason for choosing a good-looking material is that the mulch is a part of your ornamental plantings and flower beds. Salt hay, black plastic and others may be effective, but are certainly not pleasant to behold. There are too many handsome ones to choose from instead. When it comes to the vegetable garden or the berries, it doesn't matter. Salt hay is excellent.

What to mulch? All flower beds, large container plants, foundation planting—anything that you would normally have to weed and water to maintain in a healthy state. Established trees and shrubs obviously are on their own.

Which mulch material to choose? There are two considerations: cost and size of plants to be mulched. What is readily available in one part of the country will be far less expensive there than

137

in another section. Transportation plays a big part. If you have a relatively small area to cover (which you should have if you're smart), you may be able to indulge in the one mulch which appeals the most to you. Size of the plant is important because you wouldn't want to smother dainty, delicate rock garden plants, for instance, with huge stones or nuggets. Some mulches are more appropriate than others for certain areas. A wildflower garden in a naturalistic setting will look best with whatever appears to have been nature's own doing; a formal-looking mulch would be out of place. Using more than one kind of mulch in your garden prevents monotony, but don't go all out and have the place looking like a supplier's sample showcase.

How to mulch? Apply enough so that a heavy rain does not create bare spots all around, and so that weeds can't grow. Weeds reach for the light like other plants, and if they can see a tiny bit of it, they'll grow right through the mulch. A few will make it anyway, but they'll be easy to pull out. Don't bring the mulch right against the trunk or stem of a plant. This encourages rot in summer and mice-nibbling in winter. Leave a small bare ring around the plant.

In areas where nothing else grows, such as paths or patios, two mulches can be applied to make certain weeds won't grow. This is achieved by first putting down black plastic and then crushed stones or any other mulch material. You will thus avoid having to use a deadly "kill-all" herbicide periodically and worrying about some of it seeping into nearby plantings. Aisles in vegetable, herb or fruit gardens also can be treated this way.

Let's get down to mulch materials that are both attractive and effective.

Buckwheat Hulls: Soft brown in color, small, lightweight but not blown easily in the wind. Excellent for flower beds. Three inches deep will suffice. They absorb little or no moisture from the soil, yet let rainwater filter through beautifully.

Stones: Graystone chips or coarse gravel are excellent for rock garden plants. They perform two functions, helping to hold the plants down as well as conserving moisture and preventing weeds. The list of stones available for decorative mulching is long, from tiny white marble chips to crushed gravel to smooth beach rocks three to four inches in diameter. Keep in mind, however, that this type of mulching must be carefully selected to blend with the surrounding area and style of the house. Some gardens consist of little else besides the texture of natural wood set off by rocks and stone ground covers. It's not easy to rake leaves on gravel, so don't use it under deciduous trees.

Oak Leaves: Excellent, especially for azaleas and rhododendrons. If available, oak leaves are better than others because they don't mat. *Pine needles* are also very good for acid-loving plants. The advantage of leaves and pine needles is that they are very natural-looking mulches, the ones nature uses, and therefore at home in any informal garden. Adding a little lime to the leaves from time to time will prevent the mulch from making the soil underneath too acid over the years, if used on plants that are not acid-loving.

Redwood or Pine Bark: Extremely attractive, in fine texture and also in nuggets. Their brown color blends superbly with the adjoining soil. Too expensive for large areas, but worth checking availability and price in your area. The larger the bark, the deeper it must be used. Redwood does not add organic matter as it is rot-resistant.

Where looks don't matter, black plastic and salt hay are excellent, as already indicated. So are wood chips and sawdust. Peat moss dries out quickly and must be kept moist constantly. Why spend time watering a mulch when it's supposed to save you that very time in watering the bed? Cocoa-bean hulls smell of delicious chocolate when first put down, but cake in dry weather and become slimy after rain; an unattractive mold can form in damp climates. Peanut hulls, tobacco stems and ground corncobs are regional mulches that may be plentiful in your area. They're good, but not pretty.

When to mulch? In early spring when the ground is still full of moisture, and after you've fertilized the plants, where needed. After a nice, heavy rain would be perfect. Pull out all the weeds and then apply the mulch. Three to four inches deep is average, but obviously the texture and size of the mulch are the determining factors. As the mulch wears down into the soil, improving it as it does so, keep adding so that it is always at the desired depth.

12

The Gentle Art of Pruning

I know you're wondering why I should even bring up the subject
of pruning, since I have stressed throughout this book that this
chore can be eliminated if you carefully select those plants which
will not grow beyond the height you need. Pruning is time-
consuming. For this reason, clipped hedges are definitely out, as
well as carving your pet poodle out of boxwood. But one reason
you should know "how to prune what" is that you may have
inherited the task. Even though you have chosen your plant material
wisely as you *added* to your garden, that doesn't mean that you
threw out everything. Frequently, we have no choice. We have
to periodically cut back shrubs that, for one reason or another,
we have to keep.

141

Another reason for pruning applies to all plant material: dead, damaged or diseased branches (henceforth referred to as "D-D-D") should be cut off at any time of the year. Nature does it beautifully. Ever notice how, after a heavy rain or high wind, the ground is littered with twigs and sometimes branches as well? These are dead and merely needed the force of the storm to break them off. Still another reason can be called "corrective." When branches cross, they rub against each other, causing damage. Splitting, weak crotches must also be corrected.

When it comes to large trees which need pruning, cabling or bracing, call in a tree expert. You don't have the knowledge or the tools to do such a job. A tree is much too valuable an investment for you to play at being barber. Anyway, you'd end up breaking one of your own limbs instead of the tree's. Stick to small trees and shrubs. This is also true of thinning a large tree to let in more light. Don't try to do it yourself.

There are two periods when you can prune (except in the case of "D-D-D," when the sooner, the better). Plants that bloom *after* June on shoots of the current year's growth are pruned when dormant, usually in March. Plants that bloom *before* the end of June on shoots of the previous year or on older growth are pruned immediately after flowering. This is important. It divides, roughly, the spring-flowering shrubs from the summer-flowering ones.

Once you start pruning, *don't let yourself get carried away*. That is easy to do; something happens when you have pruning shears in your hands. Snip-snip clip-clip and you have a bald plant which may not make it back. Control yourself and stop every few minutes. Stand back and take a good, long look at the plant. Don't cut more than you have to.

Proper tools make your job easier—if they are cared for. You'll just gnash your teeth if you get out your pruning saw and it's so rusty you can barely move it an inch. Keep tools sharp and clean. (See the chapter on tools.) Keep a spray can of pruning paint handy and spray any plant cut that is over an inch in diameter. This will prevent disease from entering the tree via insects.

Trees

Prune them any time when the weather is not freezing. Early spring to early summer is best. However, some pruning of evergreens at Christmas-time can be done to get fragrant greens to decorate the house. That's the time of year I clip my hollies, cutting off branches that stick way out. Sometimes a tree will grow with two leaders (a leader is the central branch). Prevent possible future splitting of the tree by cutting one leader at the base of the fork or crotch. Where branches criss-cross, cut out the least important one or the one which grows inwardly, leaving the branch which grows as it should, away from the trunk. Suckers are those small twigs which grow from branches or on the trunk, or perhaps at the base.

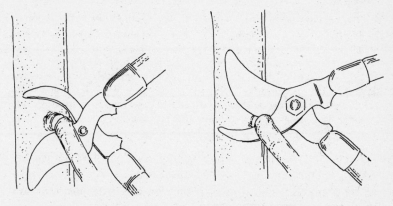

Most small limbs can easily be removed with shears or lopper; this covers branches of one to one-and-a-half inch diameter. Proper use of the tool results in a clean cut with the shortest stub possible. Drawing at left shows improper method. The limb-holder blade is at the top of the limb, while the cutting blade is under the limb. This unnatural position results in a ragged, larger stub. Drawing at right shows proper angle of tool, keeping cutting blade on *top* and as close as possible to tree trunk. Insert branch deeply into blades to get good leverage. Do not twist or try to pull limb away from trunk. This will tear the bark of the trunk and leave a messy stub.

143

Cut suckers also, as they draw valuable nourishment from the tree and will amount to nothing on their own.

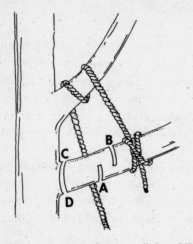

Pruning a heavy limb is not all that difficult, but a definite technique must be followed if the tree is not to be damaged—not to mention your head. The weight of the branch is too heavy to permit a single cut, flush to the trunk of the tree. The idea is to cut the branch, leaving a large stub, then cut the stub as close to the trunk as possible. To achieve this, three cuts are needed: a downcut at B and an upcut at A which will remove the limb, and a cut going from C to D to get rid of the stub. To prevent ripping of bark in really large limbs, a rope may be placed around limb to be cut—a sort of extra insurance. A sharp pruning saw is needed for this job.

Always cut as close to the main branch as possible, not leaving a stub. If the branch is on the heavy side, it may tear the bark off the trunk as it falls away. See the drawing that illustrates how to do this properly. The younger the tree, the easier to train it correctly and the less work in later years. The main idea is to remove unwanted branches before they thicken. Somehow there's always one branch that grows much faster than the others. To preserve the good looks of the tree, cut back these "over-achievers" to match the other branches. Do it judiciously, however. Keep looking at the tree from a distance to "get the picture." Remember, once cut, the branch can't be glued back. It reminds me of my hairdresser

144

and his comments on the wig that I had brought him to cut. He refused to cut off as much as I had asked him to, saying very wisely that I should wear it a few times before making that decision "because I can't put back the hair I cut off."

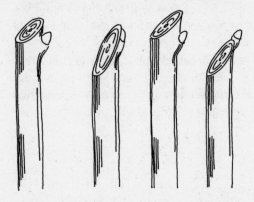

There's more to a pruning cut than just a snip of the shears. Improper cuts are shown in the three sketches from the right. The first cut is correct. The next slants too much; the one next to it is too far from the bud, while the last one is cut too close to the bud.

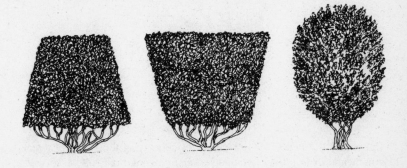

Pruning a hedge should be avoided at all cost. A hedge should be left to grow to its natural shape, as shown in drawing on extreme right. But if you must trim a hedge, the correct way is shown on the extreme left. Method shown in the center encourages weak growth at base, giving that "top-heavy" look so many hedges have.

145

Except for the usual "D-D-D," leave the evergreens alone. You'll do more harm than good by fooling around with them. Besides, most have such a handsome growth habit that they don't need shaping, unless they are terribly crowded. Then the branches that are being choked will die, and the tree will only have branches on one side—the side that has room, air and light. Nothing will make a mature evergreen tree grow new branches to replace the dead ones, so there's little you can do. Just don't get into that situation in the first place. Keep the tree's size at maturity in mind when planting. If the harm has already been done, you have two choices: transplant the youngest tree or shrub to another place

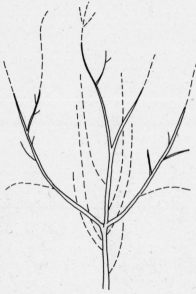

The earlier the better when it comes to controlling the shape of a small ornamental or fruit tree. Remove suckers, crossing branches, dead wood. Keep a strong leader and a few good "frame" branches that will determine the ultimate shape of the tree. Cut back, as shown, side branches and leader of young tree to encourage vigorous root system and strong framework. Function of tree determines how far from the ground lowest branches will be permitted to grow. A good rule of thumb for trees around terraces and walks is at least six feet, to prevent bumped heads and bruised guests.

if it is still small enough, or keep the best ones and cut to the ground the ones that you can't transplant for one reason or another. It's the stern law of nature that you sacrifice one in order to save the other. As in thinning seedlings, horticulture forces these "life and death" decisions on you. The survival of the fittest had its roots here (no pun intended). Fix yourself a drink, and then go out and chop that tree or shrub if it's absolutely necessary.

Shrubs

As pointed out earlier, there are spring-flowering and summer-flowering types. Evergreens make a third category. There are three main reasons for pruning shrubs; removal of "D-D-D," shaping

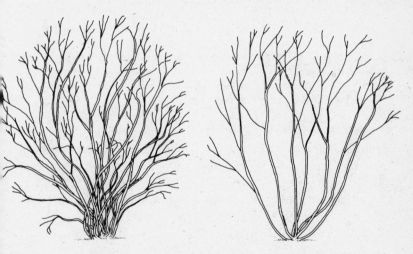

Shrubs which grow as a clump are kept young and vigorous by thinning right at the base. This means cutting old stems back to the point where they grow out of the ground. If a regular schedule is kept of cutting back one third of the clump each year, there will always be new, healthy growth and no need for drastic pruning.

(very little because you want to keep them natural and not clip them), and to promote flowering (why you selected them in the first place).

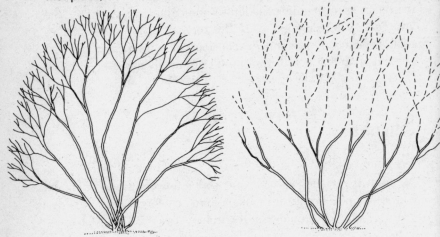

The *wrong* way to prune is to give a crew-cut to a plant. This results in new growth at the top, and still nothing at the bottom—just a lot of empty space. When a shrub has been neglected for many years, as shown on the left, drastic measures sometimes can't be avoided. Shrub should be thinned at the base, as pictured right, as well as have its top shoots trimmed back, unevenly, to give as natural a look as possible.

Don't ever, ever cut across the top of a shrub as if you were giving it a crew cut! Not only will it look ghastly, but new growth will come only from the top, resulting in a ridiculous long-legged giraffe-type shrub with a bushy head! Stems must be cut back to the ground. Thinning makes the plant bushier *all* over and also controls disorderly branches and stems. The rule of thumb is to cut back about one-third of the stems each year for three years so you can have a continuous flower show. When the time comes that the blooms get smaller and scarcer, you repeat the three-year treatment. Don't cut down everything at once.

Again, please don't let yourself go. Too much pruning and you'll reduce the number of flowers. Have in mind a firm picture of how you want the shrub to look, and then slowly, bit by bit, go about thinning it until you arrive at the desired size and shape. If you've done your homework and stick with the trees, shrubs, vines and ground covers I recommended, you won't have much pruning to do. But—if you inherited or deliberately went out (naughty you) and purchased shrubs like forsythia and lilacs (both of which I personally adore), you'll just have to pay for it. To obtain those lovely flowers year in and year out, in lush abundance, you'll have to go out there periodically and prune, my friend. But I understand and forgive you, and have described below how to do it.

Spring-Flowering Shrubs
Prune immediately after blooming.

Azalea–Remove suckers and prune branches for new growth.
Barberry (Berberis)–Just prune old wood.
Beautybush (Kolkwitzia)–Just prune old wood.
Blueberry (Vaccinium)–Remove weak twigs.
Burningbush (Euonymus)–Remove crowded branches.
Deutzia–Do the three-year bit.
Enkianthus, Redvein (Enkianthus campanulatus)–Only slight shaping, if even that, is needed.
Firethorn (Pyracantha)–Go easy if you want those beautiful berries. Prune only to control size and shape.
Forsythia–Do the three-year bit.
Honeysuckle (Lonicera fragrantissima)–Do the three-year bit, or more often as necessary to control size and promote new growth.
Hydrangea–If winter damage brings only foliage and no flowers, then wait until summer to prune, when plant normally would have flowered. Never prune in winter or early spring.
Lilac (Syringa)–Since it flowers on wood made the previous year, do the three-year renewal bit. Cut one third of the canes down to the ground. Remove all suckers.
Magnolia–Just prune to shape occasionally.
Privet (Ligustrum)–Cut four-year-old wood to the ground to promote new growth.
Rockspray (Cotoneaster)–Just prune to shape if needed.

Snowball (Styrax)–Prune to shape.
Spirea (Spiraea)–Do the three-year bit.
Viburnum–Prune to shape.
Weiglea–Prevent excessive crowding by thinning out new growth and
   pruning old branches.
Witch Hazel (Hamamelis mollis)–Prune old wood.

Summer – Flowering Shrubs
Prune when dormant, in very early spring–around
March, depending on your locality.

<u>*Abelia*</u>–Remove wild shoots. Cut out crowded branches.
Beautyberry (Callicarpa jaoenica)–Cut stems about twelve inches from
   the ground each year.
Butterfly Bush (Buddleia davidi)–Cut stems to the ground every year.
Eleagnus–Give it a "shaping" every few years.
Heather (Calluna)–Cut stems to the ground in very early spring.
Hibiscus–To get flowers, prune stems leaving two buds.
Honeysuckle, bush (Diervilla)–Prune to the ground to keep under control.
Hydrangea–Prune back this summer-flowering type to a few buds to
   cut out extra stems as necessary.
St. Johnswort (Hypericum)–To promote new growth, cut branches back,
   leaving about two buds on each branch. Cut down crowded branches.
Spirea (Spiraea)–These summer-flowering types should be cut back to
   a few buds and crowded stems removed.
Summersweet (Clethra)–Prune to shape.

Evergreens

Leave these alone if you can. Most of them only need to be pruned
because of "D-D-D" or to promote new growth. They can also
be pruned to control size and shape, but let's hope you don't have
any need to do this unless you inherited it, you poor thing! The
beauty of evergreens is their splendid growth habit and shape. There

are two kinds of evergreens: broad-leaf (like azalea and holly) and coniferous (like pine and juniper).

Prune broad-leafed evergreens any time during the dormant period (very early spring) if they produce flowers on *new* wood, meaning the *current* year. If they bear fruit, prune those after the fruit ripens. Those broad-leafed evergreens that go into their dormant period with their flower buds already formed should be pruned immediately *after* they have flowered.

Evergreens should not be pruned unless there is a very good reason for it—of course, that's true of everything else, but most especially with conifers. The four illustrations below show how pruning should be done when warranted.

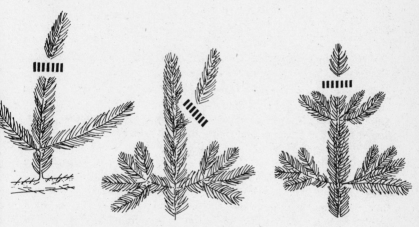

If you inherited a tree that's grown too wide for its allocated space (you'd never have made the mistake of planting it there in the first place!), you can narrow it by cutting the branches back to an inner bud. (left)

Trees should have only one strong, central leader. If two develop, select the bigger, more vigorous one, and remove the other. (center)

As spruces grow, so do open spaces between branches. This can be reduced by cutting off one-half of the terminal shoot of the leader, in the spring when new needles are not yet fully developed. (right)

151

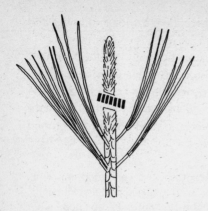

Pine needles should *never* be touched, but tree can be kept bushy and growth retarded by removing one-half of the new shoot, or "candle," in late spring.

Some broad-leafed evergreens and their requirements:

Andromeda (Pieris japonica)–Prune to promote new growth and to keep shape desired.

Azalea–Cut back leggy stems. Prune *after* flowering to promote new growth.

Box (Buxus)–Cut branches and stems; this will keep plant more compact.

Camellia (Camellia japonica and C. sasanqua)–Cut out old wood. You'll get better flowers.

Holly–Just a snip here and there to control size and shape.

Holly Osmanthus (Osmanthus)–Prune only to keep shape.

Leucothoe (Leucothoe catesbaei)–Cut down old stems if they get crowded.

Mountain Laurel (Kalmia)–Cut old stems to the ground to promote new growth.

Oleander (Nerium oleander)–Prune only to control size.

Privet (Ligustrum)–Prune to control size and shape.

Rhododendron–Prune *after* flowering to promote new growth. Cut leggy stems in early spring.

Prune coniferous evergreens—if you must—in spring when the buds and shoots are newly formed. Remember that if you want the plant to grow taller and open, you must not touch the top leader (central branch). If you cut the candle by half, you will have a shorter and denser plant. If two leaders develop, as mentioned earlier, cut out the weaker one.

Some coniferous evergreens and their requirements:

Arborvitae (Thuja)–Clip in very early spring for ragged edges and in June
for size and shape.

Fir (Abies)–Cut back candles (new shoots) about halfway to promote side
growth.

Hemlock (Tsuga)–Prune only if you must control growth.

Juniper (Juniperus)–Prune only to control growth and shape.

Pine (Pinus)–Prune only to promote new side growth (by cutting back candles halfway).

Red Cedar (Juniperus)–Cut out ragged branches in early spring and prune
only to control size in June.

Spruce (Picea)–Prune candles about halfway only to promote side growth.
Do not touch top leader.

Yew (Taxus)–Cut out ragged branches in early spring. Clip new growth
only to control size and shape.

Vines

The chief reasons for pruning vines are to cut "D-D-D" wood and
limit the size, if needed. Except for spring-flowering types, prune
all vines when dormant, in very early spring. Cut tops and branches
back as far as necessary to keep the vine under control. If space
is no problem, let her roam! In the case of flowering vines, a little
pruning each year helps to promote blooms and new growth.

13

The Borgia Shelf– Your Weapons Against the Bugs and Pests

Don't ever feel sorry for an insect if you happen to step on one. I dearly love all animals, but let me just say that trying to outwit bugs is a full-time job. I think that some actually thrive on insecticide! I have watched with fascination after spraying my greenhouse plants for white flies—spraying until I could smell it right through my mask—and making a dive for the door and a gulp of fresh air, as billowing clouds of these tiny, "fragile" monsters resumed their activities. We are now living in the era when we claim the thing to do is simply "control" insects rather than "eradicate" them. Frankly, I don't think it's so much from choice as from necessity! Who's going to admit he can't lick something that can barely be seen under a super magnifying glass?

154

Since prevention is better than having to cope with the problem later on, let's first start with what we can do to force these bugs to make their home elsewhere. Good housekeeping heads the list. Keeping flower beds clean and neat is a big help. If a plant conks out, pull it out and replace it. Broken stems and excessive amounts of dead leaves and fallen petals should be picked up periodically. Don't put your plants too close to one another. Knowing the growth habit is important here, because you do want a "lush look," yet you don't want to crowd the plants so that proper air circulation is impossible. This invites trouble.

Prune diseased parts of shrubs, vines and small ornamental trees as soon as possible. Keep the soil porous and fertile. Allow for good drainage. Buy plants which are resistant to disease. Every year new varieties come on the market which are stronger, tougher. When these are announced in the garden section of your local newspaper, jot down the names and ask your nurseryman about them.

Let's not kid ourselves that if you follow all this advice you won't get bugs. You will. Bugs *and* disease. After all, plants are living things and, like man and animals, they're prone to all sorts of problems. Fortunately, research goes on continuously to find products that control these insects and ailments. Products and state laws change, due to a very proper growing concern for our environment, so that information quickly becomes obsolete. For this reason, I strongly advise you to check with your local garden supply center before buying anything. I can give you the data only as of *this* date. Some chemicals will always be effective, the "aspirins" of the pesticide world. But why not take advantage of modern science if a brand-new formula comes out?

Before getting down to specifics, let's talk about safety. This is probably the most important information I can give you. If you forget everything else, please remember these next few paragraphs.

1. Read the label on each pesticide container *before* you open it. Read every single word carefully—even if you have to get a magnifying glass. It will tell you how much to use for which purpose

on what plants. The firm has spent a pretty penny finding this out, and the least you can do is read it. Use too much and you'll kill the plant; use too little and the bugs will laugh at you (they may anyway, but at least you'll feel righteous).

2. Dress for the part. I'm not being funny. This is important because it's virtually impossible not to get some of the liquid or powder on you somewhere or inhale the fumes, especially on a windy day (when you shouldn't be doing it in the first place, but what if a sudden breeze comes along?). You must have some old clothes lying around. A pair of jeans, a long-sleeved top, socks and sneakers are all you'll need. Cover your hair with a kerchief (I use a shower cap when no one is looking; vanity gets the better of me otherwise and I use a scarf, which isn't nearly as effective, especially in the greenhouse when the stuff drips down from the hanging baskets). Cover your eyes with a pair of ski goggles which wrap around to cover the sides as well. Finish off this appealing picture with a mask which covers your nose and mouth. This last is the only "special" item you'll have to buy which you can't use for anything else; it only costs a few dollars and is well worth it. Change the filter as directed to avoid breathing in any fumes. You won't make the centerfold of *Playboy* (or *Cosmopolitan*) in this get-up, but the possible alternative wouldn't leave you pretty either.

3. Store the pesticides on a special shelf—all by themselves, away from the reach of children and pets. Keep them in their original containers, with labels on. If a label comes off, put it back on with tape. You can't be expected to remember all the directions. Dispose of empty containers by burying them in an isolated area (away from water supplies). Chances are they won't really be "empty"; there's always a bit that remains inside. For this reason, be extra careful. Check your community authorities for designated areas where you can dispose of these containers if you can't do it on your own property. Treat it like poison—which it is.

4. If anything gets on your skin, strip and wash thoroughly with soap and water and change to clean clothing. Wash contaminated clothing and keep it for next time.

5. Don't smoke while you're spraying.

6. Last but not least: don't get lazy or complacent after doing this for some time. Don't wait until you get a scare—as I did. I decided to spray the greenhouse plants one day, after seeing a few bugs flying around—white flies, naturally. It was a sunny day and I had sunglasses on. I mixed the formula and started spraying, being too lazy to cover my hair and face. I did wear gloves, however. I was using a plastic gallon container with a narrow tube inserted in it drawing out the liquid. An adjustable nozzle controlled the spray and by squeezing the handle of the gun-like sprayer, I controlled the flow. I sprayed quickly, anxious to get it over with, and not relishing the odor anyway. I put down the sprayer to examine a plant, picked it up again and squeezed—only this time, I hadn't noticed that the nozzle pointed right at my face. I got it full on target! I panicked, dropped everything, and with heart pounding, raced out of the greenhouse—beating the world's record, I'm certain! In the kitchen I splashed cold water all over my face. After doing this, dripping wet, hair soaked, I took a shower and washed my face again, with soap and water this time. I looked at my sunglasses and thanked them profusely for preventing any of the solution from getting in my eyes. I bathed them just to be on the safe side.

Now, I again look like something from outer space when I spray, remembering vividly that terrible morning. Carelessness can exact a stiff price. Don't let your guard down.

What to use where and on what? You have to know the cause before prescribing. Insect or disease can be the culprit. In the case of insect, there are two types: chewing and sucking. The chewing ones (beetles, caterpillars, leaf miners, sawflies, borers) leave signs of their chewing behind. Bitten leaves, holes, little piles of sawdust are all calling cards. The best way of controlling them is by poisoning what they eat (without killing the plant, obviously). This is why correct measurement is an absolute must.

Sucking insects include aphids, plant bugs, lace bugs, leafhoppers, thrips, scale insects and spider mites. They pierce the surface of

157

the plant and proceed to suck out the juices. You might call them the "Draculas" of the insect world. The leaves turn yellow and curl around them, effectively protecting these pests. The best control is direct spray on their bodies—but you can see that it's a lot easier said than done. You must methodically spray the underside of the leaves if you're to get within shooting distance of them. Look for twisted, curled leaves and a silverish, sticky substance on the surface of the leaf.

There are several methods of pest control: physical, biological, through manipulation of cultural practices (such as crop rotation), and chemical. The last one is the one for us. There are many chemicals available, but unless you've always secretly wanted to play a mad scientist in his laboratory, a few will do the trick for the two major categories of insects.

For chewing insects: (* denotes trade name)
Bacillus thuringiensis preparations (Agritol*,
Bakthan L69*, Larvatrol*, Biotrol*)
Diazinon*, also sold as Spectracide*
Lindane, permitted only in certain types of preparations
Rotenone
Sevin* (carbaryl)

A few words of caution on the above. Rotenone is highly toxic to fish but of low toxicity to mammals. Sevin* is toxic to honey bees and will defoliate Boston ivy and Virginia creeper vines. Also, excessive use will cause buildup of spider mites.

For sucking insects: (* denotes trade name)
Cythion* (malathion)
Diazinon* (also sold as Spectracide*)
Kelthane* (dicofol)
Oils, dormant
Tedion* (tetradifon), substitute for Kelthane* (Good idea to alternate between the two and really fool them!)

A word on above: dormant oils should only be applied in spring,

158

and when the temperature is above 40 degrees. Check to make sure that the one you're using will not harm certain trees.

Let me repeat again, you should use any of the above pesticides only according to the manufacturer's directions. Read the label carefully in the store before buying to see that it will do the job you want, and read it again just before using to check correct proportions. Aerosols can be very effective and are great for small jobs. Again, follow directions. Systemics (Cygon* and Scope*) are only for sucking insects. By literally going through the whole plant system, they kill the insects which suck on their stems and leaves. A sneaky way to kill them, but it works!

This takes care of insects, but what about disease? If it isn't one thing it's another. Frequently, it's both. There can be many reasons for a plant to get sick: too much or too little water; too much acidity in the soil or too much nitrogen; too much lime or manganese chlorosis (anemia to you and me, yellowing of plant); chemicals in the air or soil; diseases such as virus, mycoplasma, bacterial or fungus. Now we know how "survival of the fittest" came about!

Fortunately, there are chemicals for these ailments as well. Again, knowing what to look for determines the cure prescribed. Watch for any abnormal change in the physiology of the plant (dwarfing, general or mottled yellowing, tumors, wilting, mildew, black spot). Control plant disease by watering carefully, not too much, and making sure that there is proper drainage. Provide adequate spacing and light. Remove promptly any diseased branch or other part of the plant. Buy disease-resistant plants to begin with, as already mentioned. There are all sorts of compounds that can be bought: sulfur, or fixed coppers such as Basicop*, Bordow*, Cuprocide*. Some organic fungicides are: Benlate* (benomyl), Chem Neb*, Dyrene*, Fermate* (ferbam), Fore*, Karathane*, Orthocide* (captan), Parzate, Phalthan* (folpet).

To save time, use products that do several jobs at once, such as a combination insecticide-fungicide-miticide. You can kill weeds in your lawn and feed it at the same time. Naturally, these products will cost more since the work has been done for you. You can mix ingredients yourself *if* you follow directions carefully as to what is compatible with what and how much to mix of each. The small print on the label tells you all this, and there are also spray compatibility charts available. Stick to all-wettable powders or all-liquids. To make the spray stick to the leaf, coating it thoroughly rather than running off, use a spreader-sticker in the spray solution. Check to make certain about proportions.

Lawn problems are legendary. What would most suburban dinner parties be without them in spring? They are frustration personified. Yet, as mentioned in the chapter on lawns, one shouldn't be all that fussy. When time is a precious commodity, settle for good green grass, with a few weeds thrown in. You can keep them under control rather painlessly by following a yearly schedule of feeding and weed-control. Of course, you *must* know what's causing the trouble before you reach for the bottle of chemicals. That's the rub—playing Sherlock Holmes on all fours crawling on the lawn with a magnifying glass, a few pieces of white paper and a scraper!

A quick rundown on some of the most common ailments:

Chinch bugs

Found in full sun. Look along edges of grass that has turned brown. Put down a white piece of paper and shake grass over it, or open a tin can at both ends, stick it in the ground and flood it. Watch the little bright orange or larger brown insects float!

Control: There are usually two broods a year, one in June, and another in early August which is the real killer! Apply Sevin* or Aspon* as directed. Dursban* is good for Southern lawns. Treat at the beginning of May and again the beginning of July to fight both broods. If you spot only a few bugs, one treatment in spring is sufficient.

Grubs

All kinds of beetles. Look for these *under* the roots in sunny areas, in April and early May. Treat as soon as soil is no longer frozen. Chlordane is the best control, but can be done only by professionals in some states. Better check with your local authorities. Another way to kill these pests is through application of "milky-disease" spore powder, Doom*, which has bacterial spores that kill the grubs. This, however, takes about two years to bring about—so don't be in any big hurry!

Fungi

Snow Mold: You'll spot dead areas in the grass after the snow has melted. Some patches will look pinkish, others gray. Apply before winter starts: Daconil*, Dyrene* or Fore*. *Powdery Mildew:* Found especially in badly drained areas. Control with Karathane*. *Rust:* Small, reddish spots on leaves. Control with zibeb or Fore* in late July. *Fairy Ring:* Learn to love it because there's nothing you can do about it. You and your friends can hold hands and dance around it when the moon is full. There is one way to control these rings of mushrooms (please don't eat them!) and that's by seeing that the lawn is well fertilized each year. *Leaf Spot:* Especially bad in the South. Oval-elongated brown spots of grass leaves. Control with Tersan 75* or Tersan OM*. *Fusarium Blight:* Can be the most damaging of all in the northeastern part of the country. Starts as small tan-colored spots in early summer, getting to be large areas later on. Only appears in hottest part of summer, and in warmest part of lawn. Control with Terzan OM*, Fore* or Benlate*.

For ground covers: Some weeds can be eliminated from beds of ivy and other evergreen covers through application of Dacthal*. Read directions carefully, of course, as for any chemical. This cannot be over-emphasized, especially since chemicals and their uses change literally from day to day as more is known about their effectiveness and side effects as these relate to man and his environment.

14

How Much Can You Do in Two Hours a Week: A Realistic Work Schedule

You're human. That means you're weak, a bit lazy, but you're full of good intentions. You really mean to get around to doing that special chore but the weather is just too fabulous to waste. You head for the golf course. And in bad weather—well, who can be expected to work outdoors anyway?

Schedules look great in those books that take you by the hand and keep you busy for every minute from March through November. No doubt dedicated gardeners can follow them scrupulously, skipping lunch and eating wild edible roots as they keep digging. But let's be realistic. After you've done everything that needs doing around a house—plus the end-of-week shopping at the hardware and garden supply stores, not to mention getting the car washed and picking up clothes at the dry cleaners—just how much time do you have left for gardening?

Yet, you have to squeeze some time in, somewhere. It helps if there are two of you. If you each work only two hours, it's four hours of effort achieved. Take a piece of paper and, based on the past few months' experience, jot down all the things you've done on Saturdays and Sundays—the dreary work stuff as well as the fun activities. You don't want to cut those out. That's what weekends are for, after all. Now what do you have left? One, two, three, four hours or more? This crucial little figure will determine what kind of garden you can have. Just as you know what ten dollars will buy at the supermarket, so you should realize what every hour spent in the garden will show for it.

ONE HOUR: Your weekends obviously hum with activity, that's for sure! However, you can still have a good-looking garden. It's been said that for every hour spent in the garden, you can plant thirty-six square feet. Sounds good, but thirty-six square feet of what? Shrubs? Perennials? Annuals? Vegetables? Believe me, that makes a big difference. When you have so little time, it's best to rely on maintenance-free friends such as flowering trees and shrubs, vines and ground covers. For continuous color, a bed of annuals or a grouping of containers filled with annuals will be your wisest choice. Once planted, all these can be left alone. Your one hour can be spent mowing the lawn, watering the flowers, spraying for pests, pulling out an occasional weed (you've mulched, so you won't have many), and pruning diseased or dead wood.

By far the greatest amount of time needed in a garden is in early spring, after all danger of frost has passed. This is when garden supply centers and nurseries bring out hundreds of flats of annuals and perennials, as well as of herbs and vegetables. Shrubs and ornamental and fruit trees are also displayed. A few Saturdays are given over to careful selection of the plant material you need. (You must have made a list beforehand to help you resist the temptation of buying more than you need and wondering later where to plant it!) If you've ordered anything by mail during those quiet winter

163

months, now is when it will arrive. This is also the time of year when you have to prepare the new flower beds, or pep up old ones with a shot of fertilizer. Winter storms and windy days will have left debris all over the garden. Bring out the rake and clean up the entire outdoor area. Rejuvenation of shrubs needing it (which means summer-flowering ones, not those which will flower in spring) should be done now.

You can see that the "one hour" a week will be easily taken up with routine work and planting. Maintenance comes later. One note of cheer: this busy time in the garden comes early in spring, when it's still too cold in most parts of the country to go swimming, and when the best weather is ahead for golf, tennis, sailing or just plain lazying around in the sun. The cool days are invigorating, and if you're *ever* going to be in the mood for work, it'll be then. By the time your enthusiasm has turned to fun things, all you'll have to do is straight maintenance work.

If you've selected your plant material wisely, mulched everything in sight, and put into practice all the low-maintenance tricks mentioned in this book, you can get by with only one hour a week. Many jobs have to be done only once. Just a few examples: planting trees, an evergreen hedge, vines, ground covers, flowering shrubs, hardy lilies in the pond, rock garden plants, dwarf fruit trees; putting in a mowing strip around the lawn. Perennials, carefully chosen (see list at end of that chapter), stay put for a minimum of three years. That only leaves annuals, and they're so shallow-rooted that it's a cinch to plant them. Dig a small hole, stick them in, firm the soil around them with your feet, water, mulch and that's it, until frost comes.

TWO TO THREE HOURS: Besides the bed of annuals, you can add one of perennials. Everything mentioned for "one hour" goes here as well: the cleaning up, the planting of permanent material, etc. Adding perennials means preparing the soil, planting, and, every three or four years (longer in some cases), dividing the overgrown plants. Spraying may have to be done occasionally, and cutting off dead blooms helps the plant. Let's not forget that lawns need fertilizing and application of herbicides and pesticides as required. Mulches must be added to every year to keep a minimum depth. Weeds will somehow make their way through a shallow mulch—just give them a hint of light and wow, they head straight for it!

FOUR HOURS OR MORE: That's roughly half a day. You can do a lot, depending on your grounds. Weekly mowing and maintenance of a lawn can be a small or a big job, according to its size. If you've limited the lawn area, you can spend the extra time on several flower beds, annuals and perennials. Dwarf fruit trees require weekly spraying, and you can include that in your schedule. Growing herbs is simple, once you've prepared the soil and planted them. You can add a simple "salad" garden—a couple of tomato plants and lettuce greens. Hanging baskets, window boxes and house plants summering outdoors take time to keep neat. Faded blooms are picked off, and watering is a weekly must. You can do all this, but not much more. Remember that tools are needed for all these jobs, and tools have to be kept in good working condition and put away after each use. The lawn mower needs check-ups, filling with gas and oil, cleaning. All this takes time and must be included in the hours you allot to gardening. There's more—much more—to gardening than the actual planting.

It's the little hidden things that a reluctant gardener must be on the lookout for. As with cooking, it's not just stirring the pot. There's the marketing, the preparation and all that chop-chop, the actual cooking, and then the dreary cleaning up. So with gardening. The discouraged and overworked gardener becomes that way because he tends to think only in terms of the actual "cooking." Full-time, dedicated gardeners naturally take for granted all the little "extras" needed. They're so wrapped up in what they're doing, they genuinely don't care. The golf nut who plays with red balls in the snow and has to drive two hours in traffic to get to the golf course doesn't think anything of it either—because he loves it. It's as simple as that.

No two people work at the same pace. One person may do in one hour what takes someone else two. Age, physical condition, temperament—all are important factors. The best way for you to determine what garden plan is best for *you* is to start with the minimum as described under "one hour." See how long it takes you to maintain what you already have. Obviously, don't count time spent on once-only plantings of permanent trees, shrubs, etc. It's *after* these have been done, and you've added the annuals for color, that you start keeping track of the time it takes. Then keep adding, bit by bit, until you reach the time allotment that you set for yourself. If you've gone overboard, dig up plants, give them to your friends or neighbors, put in a ground cover and forget it. It's knowing when to stop that makes the difference between a pleased, satisfied gardener—who has time to enjoy his hobbies—and a tired, bone-weary, grumpy person who isn't getting any fun and relaxation from his weekends.

Think of gardening in terms of calories. You're allowed a certain amount each day to maintain your ideal weight. Go over it, and you hate yourself. But you can eat anything you want, so long as it totals up to the right figure. You can be flexible in gardening, also. Suppose you're dying for a rock garden or lots of home-grown strawberries. No need to be frustrated. Forget flower beds (have containers of flowers around the terrace and permanent flowering shrubs) and go to town fussing over your berries or prized rock garden plants. Skip a lawn and have a ground cover of plants or attractive crushed stones or both (see photograph section). You'll find that you'll work faster and do a better job if you like what you're doing.

In an average garden for weekenders, there are basically two seasons when work has to be done to an appreciable degree: spring and fall. The spring is buying and planting time. A certain amount of pruning and cleaning up has to be done after winter. Tools are checked to see that they are in good working condition. Listing all the little chores to be done and planning the garden

166

passed time during the winter, dreaming away those long evenings in front of the fireplace. Spring is when it all gets translated into actual work.

Summer is for relaxing and minimum maintenance. This is where all that careful planning pays off. You congratulate yourself on your self-control. You admire your garden. Lush green is everywhere—trees, shrubs, ground covers, grass—the perfect background for your one or two splashes of color, the flower beds. More flowers are in containers around the terrace. Enjoy, enjoy.

Fall is a kind of mini-spring. A bit of planting is done if needed, the lawn is given extra treatment, and there's the clean-up of flower beds—pulling out dead annuals after the first frost, and cutting down perennials.

There are some chores that always need looking into. Mulch is one. This should be kept on all year, at a certain depth depending on the type used. As it gets thinned down, more has to be added. Pruning of diseased, dead or injured limbs is a constant job to be done as the need arises. Watering is a weekly must for flowers, unless nature does it for you. Until late summer, the lawn must be mowed once a week.

You now know, broadly speaking, what you can expect in terms of work to be done during the year. No two gardens are alike, so details would be futile. It's necessary to go through four seasons to get a pretty definite idea of day-to-day chores as they apply specifically to a particular property. But let me stress again that *you* determine what your property shall look like, what it will consist of, and whether it's easy to maintain or a headache. Quality in a garden is far superior to quantity. Better to have one flower bed, well tended, its healthy plants alive with color, than several beds of weedy, blah-looking things.

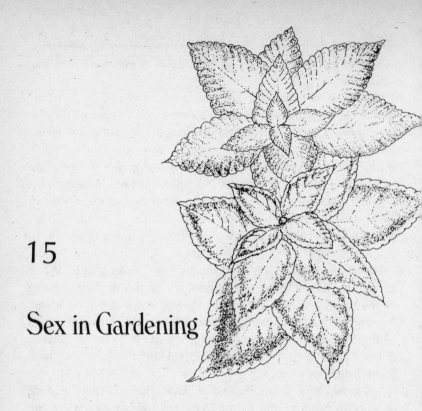

15

Sex in Gardening

Even without the flood of books to graphically remind us, we all know about sex among humans, and among animals—but among plants? The thought can become hilarious when one pictures a "boy" shrub courting his "girl" shrub. Mention this to non-gardeners (or beginners) and they think you've got nothing but sex on your mind so get thee to a shrink, but quick.

Well, they're wrong. Plants are having fun too, and you'd better know about those that need mates or which ones "produce," if you want to enjoy the results. You could sit for years staring at a sweet cherry tree, wondering when you're ever going to taste a cherry—and you won't, because it takes two, that's why. Some militant feminists, on the other hand, would love peaches, because almost all produce their own fruit without any outside help.

168

Let's get down to the birds and the bees. There are two ways flowering plants reproduce: sexually and asexually. The sexual ones are definitely sexy. They need mates to reproduce. The asexual plants are sexless, totally sterile, incapable of producing seeds. Pollination is the first step in this romantic saga of reproduction. Bees, butterflies and other insects, as well as the wind (and water among aquatic plants) are the go-betweens, carrying the pollen from boy to girl. The pollen is secreted by the male organ (stamen) and carried to the female, where it is deposited on the female organ (stigma). Immediately after contact, the pollen begins its journey downward, forming a tube which carries the sperm cell. The growth of the pollen tube terminates with the impregnation of the ovule inside the flower's ovary. The ovule then becomes the seed, and the process is finished.

All sorts of calamities can befall a plant. Sometimes it can't get fertilized because the pollen is abruptly taken away, or "embryo abortion" takes place because the plant can't give enough food to the embryo. Sometimes the embryo (seed) can't germinate because of external factors such as lack of moisture, unfavorable temperature, not enough oxygen. Think of all that next time you bite into an apple!

Sexual propagation (by seed) produces great variation, due to genetic factors. It is never true to type. On the other hand, asexual propagation (vegetative, cuttings, etc.) reproduces exactly the same plant. This is good to know only if you need more of a particular plant. Take cuttings if you want a perfect duplicate. Some plants have the ability to fertilize themselves with their own pollen. No need there to buy more than one—at least not to obtain fruit.

Apples, pears, sweet cherries and some plums must have at least two varieties of the same fruit nearby. Some apple varieties are so low-keyed sexually that they require three other varieties for adequate cross-pollination. Sour cherries, peaches (except for "J. H. Hale" and "Mikado") and small fruits (blueberries, raspberries, strawberries) pollinate themselves, so there's no worry here about mates. Currants and gooseberries like to have partners, however.

One reason for the spectacular beauty of holly is that it is covered with red berries all winter long (well, as long as the birds allow it). But you've got to have a female and a male holly to get those berries. Planted reasonably close, please. Keep that in mind when buying hollies.

Many trees and shrubs bear either male or female flowers, but not both on the same plant. These are called "dioecious." Besides the holly already mentioned, you can add Ginkgo (Maidenhair-tree), but in this case, please plant only the male tree—you *don't* want the female fruits, which have a most unpleasant odor.

The Salix family (willows) fall into the same pattern. It's the female pussy-willow that has those striking flowering catkins so highly prized by florists. Want to make your own bayberry candles? Myrica (Bayberry) usually grows wild, but you can either dig it up from its native spot or plant those that are readily bought and cultivated. *But,* whichever you do, remember that it's the female that bears the aromatic fruit, which looks grayish-waxy. When these berries are boiled, the wax melts from the fruit and comes to the surface. When cooled and skimmed, it can be made into fragrant candles.

Juniperus (Junipers) are among the most valuable of trees and shrubs—and when covered with berries they are even more beautiful. But, again, it's the female that's got them! Taxus (Yews) are popular, with good reason. And you know how you admire those brilliant scarlet berries? You've guessed right. Three cheers for the females!

There are other plants which fall into this male-female thing, but I think you get the point. When buying trees, shrubs or vines which bear flowers and fruit, ask your nurseryman about their sex habits. Don't be shy. He'll know, because he grows them. Very, very few books will tell you anything, take my word for it. Yet I feel it's important for the gardener to know that if he buys only one particular fruit tree or ornamental shrub, then he had better be prepared to do without fruits and berries, unless he's willing to buy several plants or the right sex. A rule of thumb is that one male will take care of three females. So males are important, not to mention busy! I repeat, don't make it hard for them—plant them fairly close together. It's been noticed, for instance, that dogwoods flower far more profusely when planted in clumps than when isolated. Think of that next time you look at your lone dogwood and wonder why you can count the flowers on the fingers of both hands. Maybe he or she is hankering for company.

To re-cap this sex manual: many plants have both male and female sex organs, but that doesn't mean they make use of them. Some do, and pollinate themselves; others don't, and require a few buddies around to help them. Still others are only male *or* female, and then, well, it's obvious. You need both. No diagrams for this chapter.

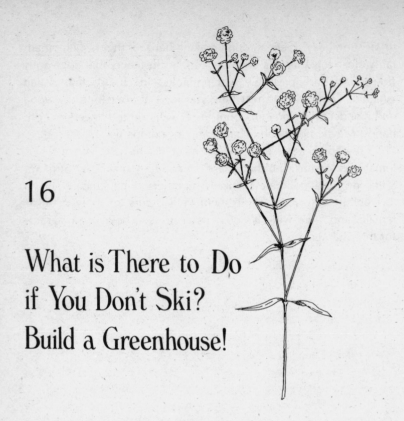

16

What is There to Do if You Don't Ski? Build a Greenhouse!

Having his very own greenhouse is the dream of the dedicated, full-time gardener. It is his "Shangri-la" in the winter. When you love doing something, you don't want to stop simply because the weather, people, circumstances, all tell you that you must. In the case of the garden nut, he wants to get his fingers in that dirt all year long.

The pleasures of gardening under glass need not be restricted to those who can give it their full time (and it sure can take just that!) by virtue of living permanently nearby. Weekenders who go to their second homes in winter as well as summer can enjoy this fun hobby too. In fact, it's practically a must if you don't indulge in winter sports. If you keep your weekend home open all year around, and you don't ski—just what are you going to do all weekend long? Sit in front of the fireplace and read? For two solid days? Stare at the bleak landscape and suggest going to a movie ten miles away? Play bridge? Make love? (The WHOLE weekend? Come on!) Sooner or later, the weekender is going to start going less and less to his retreat and stay in town unless there is something special in the country to draw him there.

I found the solution, or rather it was handed to me accidentally. Never in my right mind would I have thought of building a greenhouse. It came with the property and I was stuck with it. It looked enormous to me and was very much empty! It's an even-span model (1542) attached to a potting shed, which in turn is attached to the garage.

I did what was expected. I went out and bought lots of books on greenhouse gardening, filled with full color photographs of lush, blooming flowers and shrubs, a veritable jungle of exotica which made my head reel. I leafed through catalogs eagerly and went wild ordering dozens of plants. I became like the "sorcerer's apprentice." There was no end to it. At one point, I counted over four hundred plants. I spent literally all day Saturday and most of Sunday in the greenhouse. My husband would bring me a sandwich and a cup of coffee at lunch (we'd have a drink first), much as a St. Bernard would to a trapped victim.

I learned. It took me several years, but I learned. First, it is possible for a weekend gardener to have a greenhouse if he adopts the same relaxed attitude to indoor gardening as he does to the outdoor. He cannot expect nor should he aim for perfection. The sole reason why he should build one is to give him something pleasant to do in the winter for a few hours each weekend. It also gives him something to talk about at lunch with the boys when they tell him all about their marvelous ski weekend. He can come right back and mention that while he and his wife had their pre-dinner cocktails in the greenhouse, the fragrance from the jasmine and nicotiana was so overpowering they could hardly smell the gardenias they were cutting for the dining room table and the herbs for the salad. That's one-upmanship!

As with pets, it is essential to understand that a greenhouse demands a certain amount of *regular* attention; not much, but steady. You can't just feed a dog once in a while, and you can't water plants the same way. You—or someone else—must be available at least a couple of hours each weekend. If you're away on a short trip, all that has to be done is the watering. The rest can wait for your return.

Let's start with the type of greenhouse to build. These come in sizes to fit all pocketbooks: anything from a small one outside a window to a large free-standing model. In between are the "lean-to's," which are attached to the house. They are by far the most desirable because you can walk right into them from the house without going out in the snow and rain; you can use one as an extra "room," much like the Victorian era of solariums and conservatories; you can keep an eye on the children and what's going on in the house; you can hook up the heating system to that of the house, with a separate thermostat, and you can use the existing water lines and electricity. The only advantages in the free-standing models (away from the house) is that they get maximum sun exposure, and pesticides can be used freely without fear of getting inside the house. This model is more for the really dedicated garden hobbyist.

Depending on which wall of your house you choose to build your "lean-to" against, you can have one of several sizes. Naturally, if you choose a long wall, the greenhouse will be bigger. It should have a southern exposure for the most light, but if you can only place it facing north, you can still grow plants which require little light. The "lean-to" need not be parallel to your wall. It can be at a right angle to it, and be an "even-span" greenhouse (that means both sides of the roof are equal in size).

Do not be intimidated into thinking that all ideal requirements must be met before you can have a greenhouse built. Try to select

174

the best place, taking into consideration sun, prevailing winds (to cut down heating bills), good drainage (you don't want water seeping through the floor), and convenience (if you don't have an outside door into the greenhouse, you're in the position of city terrace people, carting bags of soil and everything else through the living room). Do have a door to the outside if you can; it will save you so much bother. It can be located at either end of the greenhouse— preferably at the end facing a path or an open area where a wheelbarrow can be brought right up to it with pots, fertilizers, potting mix, etc.

Keep in mind that your greenhouse need not be earth-bound. You can have it built off your second floor, on a roof extension. The window of your bedroom becomes a door to your greenhouse. To combat the convenience problems described above, you should limit yourself to smaller plants that will not necessitate the mess of large transplanting and the materials needed for such a chore. This type of greenhouse would be more of a decorative solarium, but a lot of fun and satisfaction. Think of having breakfast there while reading your morning paper!

Unless you are a do-it-yourself whiz kid, do not attempt to build the greenhouse yourself. Such problems as foundations, water pipes, ventilation systems, etc. are really quite involved. Select an expert in greenhouse building, and select the model you want with his advice. A greenhouse should get at least three to four hours of sun a day. The even-span model should have its ends face north-south or east-west. If the ends of the greenhouse face north and south, all the plants will get some sun during the day; if the ends face east and west, the plants on the north side will always be shaded.

Every greenhouse needs a foundation, however low, as in the "down to the ground" greenhouses with glass all the way to the floor. The foundation should match or complement that of the house, if it is attached to it. Go over this with the builder. As for flooring material, I prefer bricks because they absorb water beautifully, and release moisture slowly afterwards. Others prefer wooden slats, because they're warmer on your feet, for one thing. During the colder winter months I place plywood on the brick floor of the two aisles of my greenhouse. This gives me the best of each! When the warmer weather comes, I just pick up the two long wooden slabs and place them under the benches until the following winter. But use your imagination in selecting the flooring. If the greenhouse is going to be used extensively as a second living room, consider flagstones or any material that one would use on the terrace. So long as it can be hosed down, and drains properly, you can use anything.

You will be told that "everything is automated" these days, and that you can have a greenhouse that will think for itself when you're not there and do all your chores for you. Believe it only to a certain point. *If* you are going to be there all week, then by all means invest in all the mechanical gadgets you want. If they go berserk (and they do, you know) or there's a power failure, you're around to prevent a disaster—such as the sprinkler getting stuck and not shutting off, among other things.

Now I'll readily admit that this is a personal quirk of mine. I don't trust machines very much. I still feel funny leaving the house with a roast in the oven, hoping it will shut itself off as it's supposed to. We've all heard stories about machines getting even with people and doing crazy things, haven't we?

However, what I'm advocating won't exactly put you back in the Stone Age. First, you'll have a thermostat. Whatever temperature you select, that's what you'll get. It will vary, however, in different parts of the greenhouse. You'll notice, if you place several thermometers around, that you will get some "cold" spots. That's good. That's where you'll put the plants that need a lower temperature.

There are three types of greenhouse "climates" you can have. Imagine, creating your own ecology! A "cool" greenhouse means *night-time* temperature of 45 to 50 degrees; the "intermediate" greenhouse is 50 to 55 degrees; and the "warm" greenhouse runs from 60 to 70 degrees. In spring and fall, when the sun shines on the glass, it can go well over 100 degrees—and that's when it's only about 50 degrees outside!

The temperature you select will depend on the plants you wish to grow. You are allowed a certain leeway because of the "cold pockets" already mentioned, but not terribly much. You cannot mix tropical plants and alpines. Stick to plants that will thrive within the same temperature range. As there is enormous choice in any of the three temperature zones, you needn't worry about monotony of plant material. Also, you'd be surprised at how well plants adapt! I shouldn't admit this, but my greenhouse is my winter version of my summer "Russian roulette" garden. I set the thermostat at 60 degrees, and it more or less keeps the faith. Cracks in the insulation, and our not-so-great heating unit, do not make for uniform heat. Nothing is mechanized, so that humidity and vents depend on me. On weekends, I hose down the brick paths and under the aisles to create moisture, and open the top vents according to the latest long-range weather forecast for the coming week. If that's not gambling! Yet, I have flowers all winter long, take and grow cuttings of same at any time, and have relatively few failures. But I do not have rare, delicate, "exotic" plants, which is the answer. Even my orchids are the sturdy types, for cooler temperatures.

"Survival of the fittest" is really the key to successful gardening in a greenhouse when the owner is absent five out of seven days. You will soon find out which plants are impossible to kill—they will take drops in temperature (due to power failures), haphazard humidity, and once-a-week, twice at the most, watering. So many of the same principles which apply to outdoor gardening go for indoors. Don't knock yourself out trying to grow plants that stubbornly won't produce for you. Keep good sanitation habits (which is the outdoor version of neat housekeeping inside). Pick dead leaves, keep the greenhouse floor and benches clean, space plants for proper air circulation, and isolate or throw out diseased plants.

There are four components needed to create your own greenhouse climate: heat, water, light, air. You can control heat via your thermostat. Come the warm spring sun rays, excessive heat will build up. This can be cut down by putting up shades on the glass roof and sides. Permanent ones are available, as are roll-up bamboo shades which I use because I prefer the way they look. They last only about two years, but are very inexpensive. Whitewashing the glass is messy-looking and best left to commercial growers. As a week-end gardener you would be wise in the summer to take all the plants from the greenhouse, grouping them attractively outdoors. This saves installing expensive air conditioning and gives you an opportunity to repaint, fix up and clean the greenhouse, making it ready for the first cold days of fall (*before* first frost when you'll bring all your little darlings back in).

Water is a component less easy to control. First of all, even if you were there full time to take care of it, you couldn't have an automatic water sprinkler unless you grew only the same kind of plants—all needing precisely the same amount of moisture. When one does under-glass gardening for fun, who wants to limit oneself to nothing but carnations, or geraniums, or begonias? The pleasure is in growing a variety of plants, especially at first, until you determine what you really like, and what will thrive best. Each pot has to be watered individually according to its needs. That's how they do it in botanical gardens. Also, steady overhead watering, however misty, encourages all sorts of diseases, as opposed to watering at the surface of the pot.

However, there are a few ways to "beat" the watering problem, or at least to keep it fairly under control. You'll soon find out which plants are the "camels," requiring little water, and which are the "drinkers." After you've thoroughly watered each pot so that the water comes out the bottom, go back to the "drinkers," place a rubber or plastic saucer under the pots, and fill them with water. The plants will draw water as they need it during the next few days. If they are "heavy drinkers," the roots won't have time to rot. If you're in doubt, add a layer of pebbles at the bottom of the saucer. Barely cover them with water, and then place the pot on top. Or insert any one of several gadgets on the market. One consists of a batch of "spaghetti" wicks, one of which is inserted in each pot; all the wicks are connected to a pail of water, and each plant draws what it needs. This capillary method of watering

178

is an old one and fairly good. Another trick is inserting a plastic "bulb" in each pot. This is also based on capillary action in that the bulb-like "ball," which is filled with water, releases only what the plant needs. Large tubs will require two or more of these to do a good job. However, nothing is perfect. These measures are only helpful aids.

Another trick to retain moisture in pots is to use plastic ones only. Although clay pots are better because they are porous, moisture seeps out quicker for that very reason. Plastic pots have their disadvantages, but for the weekend gardener who can only water once or twice a week, water retention has top priority. Keeping a mulch of sphagnum moss or pine bark on the larger pots and tubs is also helpful. When it comes to small pots, these can be grouped together in a "vermiculite" moisture bed. All this means is filling a plastic pan with vermiculite, getting it good and wet (it retains moisture beautifully), and then setting pots right into it. Make it deep enough for the vermiculite to come about one-quarter up the pots. The drainage holes at the bottom of the pots will take in the moisture as needed.

However, I want to stress that such measures as outlined should only be used on those pots that you *know* dry out thoroughly a few days *before* your arrival. Better to let them dry out just a bit too much than to overwater. I have often looked at a sadly wilted plant, fearing the worst, only to have it back in full health a mere hour or two after watering it thoroughly.

One thing more: if your greenhouse is a "lean-to" model, you will have both hot and cold water lines available to you. This means you can mix the water to a nice, tepid temperature which plants love. But don't panic if only cold water is what you can use. My greenhouse, being located away from the house, has no hot water. This means that all winter long I use cold water on my plants. Nothing horrible has happened as a result. (My husband uses the *ice water* from the water cooler in his office to water his plants, and all I can say is that they are flourishing—not to mention that he likes an ice-cold office and the air conditioner is on from April to November. So much for "rules.")

It is nearly impossible to control humidity in a greenhouse when you are not around, and when automatic devices are not used. The best you can do is to hose down the floor and the benches just before you leave. My benches are filled with small pebbles which retain moisture very nicely. On hot, late spring days when the sun shines, I can only hope for the best. That's when I put up the bamboo shades.

Light can be adjusted, as already mentioned, by the use of shades. You should know approximately when the temperature starts zooming during the day, yet drops sharply at night, in your part of the country. This is when the glass should be shielded from those hot rays. Shades will cut down on the light, but will prevent your plants from cooking. Flowering plants need far more light than foliage ones, so group them together accordingly. There is always one spot in the greenhouse which gets more light. As with temperatures, you have "light" drops also.

Shade-loving plants should be placed under hanging baskets or under large shrubs. I keep a giant rubber tree as well as other tall plants for that purpose. These form built-in "parasols" for plants which do not like much sun. A canopy of hanging baskets does the same trick. Sun-loving pots can be placed on glass shelves lining the glass walls and right around the outside of the benches near the wall. Through trial and error you will know where certain plants thrive. You could install fluorescent tubes to increase the light in the greenhouse, but leave that to the pros and hobbyists. As a weekender, you must do the reverse of what might be considered the norm: grow those plants that will do well under the conditions prevailing in your greenhouse, rather than make your greenhouse suit the cultural requirements of the plants. Only elaborate and sophisticated automatic equipment can produce the latter.

Air is not too difficult to control—if you listen carefully to the

180

long-range weather forecasts, look up at the sky, and come to your own conclusion as to what the next seven days will bring! A greenhouse must have a certain amount of fresh air circulation, even in the middle of the coldest winter. I always have the ceiling vents open, even if only one or two inches. An air-tight greenhouse invites pests and diseases. So long as the air does not blow directly on the plants, you can safely keep a vent of window open a crack. Only in this one area would I trust an automated system. If the worst should happen—a power failure just when the vents are open at their widest—it would take quite a long time before the inside of the greenhouse would become so cold as to freeze the plants.

The principle of automated vents is quite simple. When the temperature goes up past what is set on the thermostat, the gadget which is hooked up to the thermostat (set for highest and lowest temperature) will automatically close or open the vents as the needs warrant it. There are also non-electric automatic vent openers. These are cylinders filled with gases which expand as the temperature goes up. They "push" a rod which in turn is connected to the ventilators. Neither model should be hooked up to windows or ventilators which are capable of opening to an extreme degree. Limit what your "absentee brain" can open, to be on the safe side. My greenhouse is totally manually operated and this "weather gambling" on my part has been going on for quite a few years now, and nothing traumatic has occurred.

Only professional growers are in a position to combine perfectly the four elements of water, heat, light and air in a greenhouse. Don't try it. You can still get beautiful results with your own home-made techniques. Buy two good thermometers and hygrometers made for greenhouses and these will indicate the spots where temperature and humidity change.

What will you need for your greenhouse—besides plants? This, of course, depends on how large it is, how much use you wish to make of it (such as propagation of existing plants), and whether or not you have space adjoining it to hold equipment and do your "work." Let's just take the minimum. Suppose you have a "lean-to" model with a bench running along the three sides. The fourth side is the wall of the house. The greenhouse door opens right into the house, so there is no room for a potting shed or workroom. This means taking over one of the short sides of the greenhouse as your working area. The bench is the flat surface you'll need to do the potting, etc. Under the bench you can have several tall plastic containers (garbage cans are great, as they have covers), in which you keep your different mixes: one for potting soil (which you buy in 25 or 50-lb. bags), one for peat moss, one for vermiculite, and one for perlite (or one for builder's sand in place of the last two, if you prefer and are able to get it). Smaller plastic cans can hold bonemeal and limestone. These are all ingredients that will go into the potting mixtures for your plants.

You will also need a container for broken clay pieces (obtained by breaking old clay pots) to use as drainage material. Have a smaller plastic container for coarse sphagnum moss (see Chapter 9). Also under the benches you will need to stack the pots of different sizes—all plastic (so you don't need to water as often, remember). One or two rectangular plastic trays to hold cuttings should round out this basic list. A garbage can to hold "real garbage" should also be available. Into this will go diseased plants, old soil that may have bugs in it, cracked plastic pots, etc.

A water faucet with a plastic hose attached to it is an obvious must. It will probably be on the house wall, connected to the regular pipes. You may have both hot and cold water, so have a double couplet that will let you mix that tepid water plants prefer. Coil the hose on a metal holder made for that purpose. Get a soft, flexible plastic hose that you can squeeze and "double up" easily. With a regular nozzle head at the end, you have all you need to do your watering. By "squeezing" the hose, you can get down to a trickle for a tiny pot, or by "letting go" you can water deeply a large tub. Don't hang baskets so high that you can't reach comfortably to water them. Besides, you want to be able to stick your finger in them to feel if they need watering. Not to mention that you want to admire them without pulling a neck muscle. A small shelf can hold your fertilizers and spray cans for pest control.

As for tools, these are pretty modest in number. For this reason (among others), buy the very best. You won't regret it. You'll save money in the long run because you won't have to replace them nearly so often, and they'll do a far better and easier job for you. Stick to stainless steel whenever possible. It won't rust in the moist atmosphere of a greenhouse. You'll need a sharp knife (for taking cuttings), a pair of scissors (for snipping off faded flowers, etc.), a small hand pruner (to prune the heavier shrubs), a cultivator (a tool that resembles a hook to scratch the top of the soil in pots), scoops for the potting mixture cans, one or two trowels, and gloves.

Do you have a lot of old ice cube trays? You know how the cube separator just won't work properly after a while, and you're left with a perfectly good tray? I've got dozens! Well, just fill it halfway with vermiculite, wet thoroughly, and place your small pots inside so they can draw the moisture during the week. Save the larger plastic trays already mentioned for large pots.

What kind of plants you grow in the greenhouse depends, obviously, on many factors. However, since you'll take them out during the summer, I would suggest that you grow two basic kinds: (1) plants that you will use in the flower borders (money saved!) and (2) plants that you will keep in their containers as "show off" plants around the terrace.

Before the first frost kills your annuals, dig up your favorites, but be merciless—only those that look the strongest and healthiest. Pot them and cut them back, which means you'll have cuttings. Do this gradually and by the time you are ready to start the flower bed again, you will have a good supply on hand. You may end up having all you'll need!

As for "show off" plants, your personal taste and the temperature of your greenhouse are the only major factors to consider. A small gardenia plant given to you at Easter can, in a few years, become an impressive shrub. Any plant that can be trained to grow in a single stem can be made into a "standard." Forcing spring bulbs weeks before they would make their first appearance outdoors brings cheer when there is still snow and ice on the ground. The greenhouse can be a source of plants for your city apartment. When these start to look a bit "weak," you simply bring them back for a rejuvenation period in the humid atmosphere of the greenhouse.

As with outdoor gardening, I would strongly advise against growing anything from seed. Again, it is a matter of *constant* moisture to bring about germination. Plastic bags and all, this is still risky business. Keeping cuttings moist is far easier, and gives good results. I save the plastic trays, the ones with holes at the bottom that serve as containers for annuals that are sold in flats. I line the bottoms with paper towels, then fill the trays with vermiculite (perlite is not good as it dries out completely), and water them thoroughly. I put the cuttings in this mixture (after dipping them in a hormone powder to hasten root formation and prevent stem rot). Six of these small trays are placed inside one large plastic tray. This tray is filled with water about one-third from the bottom. During the week, the small trays with cuttings will draw additional moisture from the large tray as needed. All the water has usually disappeared by the time I look at them again the following Saturday.

By lifting a cutting carefully, you will know if it has roots and is therefore ready for potting. If the cutting comes out easily, put it back for another week. If it "resists" when you gently try to pull it out, you know that the roots are there, hanging on! Use a tablespoon or small scoop to lift it out, and then pot it.

The three basic potting mixtures are given in the chapter on "Container Gardening." As mentioned there, instead of builder's sand which you must add to the loam (soil), you can substitute half vermiculite and half perlite. It's far easier to buy ready-mixed potting soil, to which you add the necessary ingredients, than it is to dig out dirt from your garden, sift it, and then bake it in your oven in order to sterilize it. Certainly not after you finally blew the family's budget by buying a super deluxe self-cleaning oven to get rid of dirt!

184

Insect and disease control inside a greenhouse is virtually the same as outdoors (see the special chapter on this subject). However, because you are confined indoors, you must double your caution in handling chemicals. Inhaling the fumes and having some of the pesticides drip on you from hanging baskets are factors which are far more serious indoors than out. For this reason, buy two things: a respirator which covers your nose and mouth filtering the air you breathe in, and a pair of ski goggles which completely cover your eyes, sides as well. If you don't mind looking like something from outer space or ready for Halloween calls, add to these items a plain shower cap to cover your hair completely. (Actually, the kids will think you're real "cool" looking!)

Many plants benefit from being cut back, especially after being brought in from a summer outdoors. As stated earlier, this in turn gives you the opportunity of taking cuttings. Select the healthiest tips of a plant, vigorous new growth if possible, and cut one about two inches from the tip. Snip off and discard any flowers or flower buds. Dip it in hormone powder and insert it in your propagation medium.

Since an entire book could be written on greenhouse gardening alone (and many excellent ones have been), I can only give you some highlights in this chapter to whet your appetite and show you that it's not all that difficult. Buy one of these books and you'll fast become knowledgeable. Keep in mind, however, that these books are written for people who garden *every day* or at least are on the spot. Don't get carried away. It can become a tremendous job. As in owning a boat, the thousand and one chores that go into the maintenance are never written about, but they exist! So build as large a greenhouse as you care to, but go easy at first on filling every square inch of it with plants. Start with a modest collection, learn how to handle this, get some experience, and then add little by little as your *free* time allows. It's winter, so you'll have more of it; then comes summer with golf and the rest to tempt you!

Technically, if given the precisely duplicate climate environment of its native habitat, any plant that grows outdoors will grow indoors. But we all know that this abracadabra is nearly impossible for the professional, and a fantasy for the weekend gardener. There are certain plants that are sturdier than others which will "produce" for you. I offer a brief, partial list to get you started. Don't be afraid to experiment. It's through trial and error that you will learn which plants are for you.

Since the temperature in your greenhouse will vary from one corner to the other and most plants adapt quite nicely to a mild increase or decrease in temperature, I have listed plants according to only two categories: a "cool" greenhouse and a "warm" greenhouse. The "cool" has a night temperature ranging from about 45 to 59 degrees, the "warm" from 60 to 70 degrees. Do not be too concerned, however. Many plants do well in both types of environment, unless you go to extremes in coolness or heat. Mine is roughly a 60-degree greenhouse and I mean *roughly!* Yet I grow all sorts of plants. The trick is to know *where* to place your plants. So use the plants I have listed below with *flexibility*. (Remember, they can't read!)

Plants for the "cool" greenhouse
(all in pots, naturally)

Acacia (Acacia armato)
  (A. Drummondii)
Alyssum (Alyssum maritimum)
Anemone (Anemone coronaria)
Begonia (tuberhybrida)–Tuberous Begonia
  (B. semperflorens)–Wax Begonia
Camellia (Camellia Japonica)
Cape-Primrose (Streptocarpus wendlandii)
Cyclamen (Cyclamen indicum)
Ferns (Adiatum pedatum and A. cuneatum, "Maidenhair," among others)
Flowering Maple (Abutilon)
Freesia (Freesia hybrida)
Fuchsia

Geranium (Pelargonium)–(4 categories: Zonal, the most popular; Lady Washington, pansy-like flowers, gets leggy; Scented-leaved, many fragrances; Ivy-leaved, great for hanging baskets and window boxes.)
Kalanchoe (Kalanchoe Blossfeldiana)
Orchid (Cymbidium genus)
Primrose (Primula malacoides)
    (P. Sinensis)
Sweet Olive (Osmanthus fragrans)

Good for Hanging Baskets and/or Vines:

English Ivy (Hedera Helix)
Jasmine (Jasminum officinale)
    (J. Sambac)
Kangaroo Vine (Cissus antarctica)
Kenilworth Ivy (Cymbalaria muralis)
Leadwort (Plumbago)
Philodendron (Philodendron cordatum)
Sprenger Asparagus Fern (Asparagus Sprengeri)
Strawberry Begonia (Saxifraga sarmentosa)
Tuberous Begonia (Begonia tuberhybrida)–hanging variety
Variegated Periwinkle (Vinca major variegata)
Wax-plant (Hoya carnosa)

Plants for the "warm" greenhouse:

(all in pots)

African Violet (Saintpaulia)
Amaryllis (Hipeastrum aulicum)
Aspidistra (Aspidistra lurida)
Azalea
Wax Begonia (Begonia semperflorens)
    (B. Rex)
    (B. socrotana)–Christmas Begonia
Cacti and Succulents in varieties
Coleus (Coleus blumei)
Croton (Codiaeum variegatum pictum)
Daffodil (Narcissus)

Dieffenbachia in varieties
Ferns–Davallia and Asplenium in varieties
Freesia (Freesia hybrida)
Geranium (Pelargonium)
Gloxinia
Hyacinth (Hyacinthus)
Hygrangea (Hygrangea macrophylla)
Impatiens
Kalanchoe (Kalanchoe Blossfeldiana)
Lantana
Orchid–Cattleya, Cypridedium, Denbrobrium (intermediate heat)
   Phaelenopsis, Vanda, Coelogyne (over 65 degrees at night)
Peperomia (Peperomia obtusifolia)–green and variegated
Philodendron
Rubber Plant (Ficus elastica pandurata)
Tuberose (Polianthes tuberosa)
Tulips (Tulipa)

Good for Hanging Baskets and/or Vines:

Allamanda (Allamanda carthartica Williamsii)
   (A. Neriifolia)
   (A. Violacia)
Black-eyed Susan (Thumbergia alata)
Bougainvillea (Bougainvillea spectabilis)
Browallia (Browallia speciosa major)
Passion Flower (Passiflora grandiflora)
Rosary Vine (Ceropedia Woodii)
Star Jasmine (Trachelospermum jasminoides)
Stephanotis (Stephanotis floribunda)–Madagascar Jasmine; does well in
   both cool and warm greenhouses
Wandering Jew (Tradescantia zebrina)
   (T. multiflora)

17

Tools -- Friend or Foe?

We all make the same mistake when we first start to garden. We go out and buy far too many tools—the wrong kind, and certainly not the best quality. A few years later, we sadly clean out the garage, throw out a pile of rusted, broken tools—some used only once or twice—and begin all over again.

We're wiser now. We've learned that tools can sabotage our work or make it infinitely easier. Ever try to saw even a small limb with a dull saw? You might as well be cutting down one of those giant Sequoias in California redwood country for the effort that it takes. Buy only what you need for specific jobs in mind. Buy the very best quality that you can afford. In fact, you can't afford not to, as it will cost you less in the long run.

Where to store tools depends on your property. If you have room to build a small tool house, screened from view by an evergreen hedge or covered with an attractive vine, you're in luck. Most of us have to rely on the good old garage. After all, you've got three walls there just begging to be put to use. Nail a strip of pegboard about four feet wide along the walls, and you can hang up an amazing number of tools. Use the type of pegboard hooks that are screwed in tightly; otherwise, every time you take a tool off, the hook will drop at your feet. Use plenty of hooks and place them so that the tools will be held securely. Nothing like having a rake fall on your head to make you wish you hadn't rushed the job. Remember, you'll only do it once. There's no need to create a pop art mural. You'll never put back a tool in precisely the same spot. You'll start out that way, admiring the whole pleasing effect of tools decoratively hanging on the walls, but believe me, give it two or three weeks of use—and it won't be the same. But at least the tools will be *hanging* and off the floor.

When you invest in good tools you don't want to lose them, and you must keep them in good shape. Paint bright orange stripes on the wooden handles so that they'll pop right out of the grass or wherever you left them when you went to answer the telephone. Bright adhesive tape does the same trick where paint is not feasible. Keeping tools clean can be a great big bore which we'd just as soon forget about. One way to make this chore easier is simply to fill any container with at least one foot of sand that has been saturated with crankcase oil. The sand acts as an abrasive which cleans the tool of soil and dirt, and the oil leaves a thin coat on the tool, preventing it from rusting. When you walk into the garage, just stick the tool in, push-pull a couple of times, and that's it.

A basic list of tools for specific jobs should include:

1. A *spade* (square-sided) and a *shovel* (pointed-nosed) for digging holes to plant shrubs, small trees, large clumps of perennials, and for lots of other uses.

2. A *spading fork*—a must in transplanting since it doesn't cut roots as would a shovel or spade. It's also needed to spread salt hay.

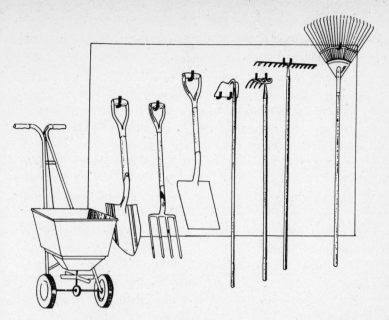

From left to right: Rotary spreader, shovel, spading fork, spade, hoe, cultivator, steel garden rake, lawn rake.

3. An ordinary *hoe* to cultivate flower and vegetable beds and to break up small clumps of soil in early spring.

4. A *cultivator* with three- or four-pronged teeth. It loosens the soil nicely, and mixes ground fertilizer in soil around plants.

5. *Hose.* Use lengths of up to 50 feet; more becomes too hard to use and store. Each hose should have its own nozzle head and storage basket or wooden tub. The latter is better as it will stand up to the weight of the coiled hose. Place these wherever you have an outside faucet.

6. *Sprinkler.* Unless you have an automatic, underground sprinkler system (a terrific idea if you have lots of lawn), you will need one or maybe two of these, which you can use simultaneously. This is primarily for keeping grass seed moist in areas that need it. Unless you are prepared to water deeply and regularly, it is best to leave the grass alone.

7. *Soil soaker.* This is nothing more than a length of hose with holes in it, or one made of canvas so water can seep out slowly

and gently. This is used to water flower beds, shrubs, anything that might suffer from overhead watering.

8. A *trowel*—a good all-steel one. It's indispensable for planting flowers and vegetables, or anytime a small hole is needed.

9. A *pruning saw*—the curved kind for smaller limbs. You should wait until you've mastered this one before buying a bigger model with coarse teeth used for cutting large limbs.

10. A *pruning lopper*—this cuts branches that are too small to require a saw.

11. Drop-forged *pruning shears*—as indispensable as a trowel. They do a million jobs! Cut any small branches of shrubs, twigs, woody plants. Buy the best you can get. They'll make any job seem like cutting butter.

12. *Extension pruner.* It's really a combination lopper and saw (it comes with both) to cut small limbs that are too high to reach. Far safer than climbing a tree (resist that childish temptation) or swaying on a ladder.

13. *Hedge shears.* I almost hate to list them, as so much damage is done with them. However, if you have a small hedge that you must keep trimmed, this is the tool for you.

14. *Sprayer.* Many kinds are available, but unless yours is a large estate, the "trombone" kind is best and easiest. Also good is the gallon jug model with squeeze handle that has a nozzle to adjust spray from fine mist to powerful spray. Get two sprayers, one for regular pesticides and one for the real "killer" chemicals that are meant to eradicate totally whatever they touch, as when you spray a driveway for weeds. You know you won't take the time to thoroughly disinfect the sprayer after each use, so get two. With paint, mark one with a big "X" so you know it's strictly for the deadly stuff. The knapsack sprayer is only for men—with stout backs. Sprayers that attach to garden hoses are easy to use, but not too good if your water pressure fluctuates, as this is the determining factor in the correct proportion of chemical and water.

15. *Lawn mower.* If yours is a rocky, uneven lawn, then the rotary model is better than reel, although the latter does a neater job. If you have a large area, by all means invest in a rider model.

You'll save hours of toil and the vibration from the seat will save you the weekly work-out at the Y.

16. A *wheelbarrow*—no need to explain why this is needed. Also, get one of those *carts* with large rubber wheels. They'll carry far more than the traditional wheelbarrow with less effort.

17. Plastic *pails* for mixing fertilizers. Get the two-gallon size, marked accordingly so you can measure correctly.

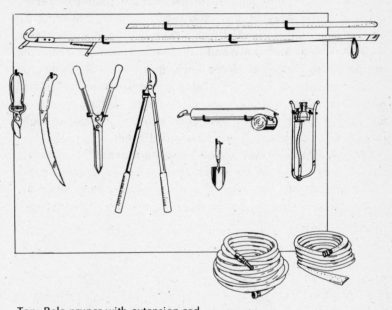

Top: Pole pruner with extension rod.
Below, left to right: Drop-forged pruning shears, pruning saw, hedge shears, pruning lopper, sprayer for small jobs, trowel, oscillating sprinkler.
Bottom, left: Garden hose with nozzle. Right: Soil-soaker.

This list should see you through just about any garden jobs. As you go along, the need for a special tool may come up. Wait until then to buy it. If you're going to plant one hundred daffodil bulbs, by all means get one of those bulb planters, but a good trowel will do the same job—the hole just won't be perfectly round!

Power tools, except for the lawn mower, can easily be rented, unless you find you have steady use for them. First of all, as with spray pesticides, they are to be treated with kid gloves. They are lethal weapons and take expertise to use. One careless motion and you're minus a finger. If you're unfortunate enough to have a long hedge that must be kept trimmed, then obviously a power hedger is for you. Mowing strips eliminate the need for edging, so there's no need for that tool.

A leaf blower is a big help in the fall and should be rented if you are in a wooded area. You need use it only twice: once when the ground is covered with leaves, and then a few weeks later when they are all down and you do a final clean-up. Thatching machines are also good for the lawn, if you need to do this job on a large scale. If you have a bank or similar extensive area to till prior to planting ground covers or shrubs, renting a rototiller will save you tremendous labor. Look into all these power tools, but don't buy them unless you have a real need.

With your lawn mower and all power tools, read the manufacturer's instructions carefully as to maintenance. The better care you take of these tools, the longer they'll last and the more efficiently they'll perform. Store them in a dry place and keep them covered, out of the way.

18

When a Green Thumb Turns Red

Well, it will, you know—sooner or later. All sorts of accidents happen to new gardeners, and sometimes to experienced ones too! You've already read about safety measures with pesticides, when pruning, and when using tools, especially power tools. What I want to add now is chiefly for people living way out in deep country, or in the woods, or far away on a lonely beach—in brief, far from a doctor or hospital emergency room.

Now, you may not be the neurotic I am, and won't give thought to emergencies that can happen around home and garden. Well, I do. And, to add to my shame, I happen to be near a fine hospital. Oh, well—so much for my hang-ups. However, don't wait until you become a victim—please take these basic precautions.

Buy the Red Cross First Aid Handbook—the best of its kind and indispensable. Most doctors don't know as much about first aid themselves. They're far beyond that sort of thing, don't you know. Next, find out if you're allergic to certain bugs or plants. Get the necessary shots, for goodness' sake. Keep a bottle of pills for bee sting should you prove to be allergic and not know it. There you would be, in the middle of nowhere, miles from any living soul, and suddenly a bee or yellow jacket stings you and you start to swell up—among other things too ghastly to describe. Swallow a little pill and you'll be all right. Worth having on hand, wouldn't you say? The same is true of tourniquets, first aid materials, and phone numbers of the nearest hospital and emergency poison control station (to cover snake bites).

Above all, don't lose your head. This way you'll remember what you've read or heard—which can be of great help. I should know. I was walking by the greenhouse one Sunday morning when I heard a funny, whining-in-pain sound in the pachysandra bed nearby. As I got closer, I could see a small animal, but it didn't move. I inched nearer, and saw the cutest baby rabbit. Naturally, picked it up gently, and it didn't move in my arms. I was so enchanted (and so green at this gardening and great outdoors stuff) that I asked my husband to run back to the house and get the camera to take a shot of dear bunny rabbit. By the time he got back, "dear bunny rabbit" was getting quite restless, and as I held him in my arms and my husband snapped a "corny picture," bunny rabbit sank its teeth into my hand, good and proper. My Red Cross training came to the fore, and remembering all the things that rabbits can have (rabies being the major offender, who needs any other!), I also remembered reading about *keeping* the animal that bit you—if you can capture him (good luck to you). In a calm frenzy, I informed my husband that we had to capture the rabbit which I had dropped when he bit me. This we did in a pitifully easy way—the poor thing was so sick it couldn't move quickly.

The hospital gave me some injection, the police took the animal to the state's laboratories to test it for rabies, local radio stations and newspapers used me as an example of what *not* to do (pick up and handle wild animals), and I was having a nervous breakdown waiting for the results of the test. I visualized Pasteur and all the gory belly injections. Fortunately, it all ended well, but for the rest of the summer I was "that rabbit nut" of the village. At the beach, the local policemen would wave a cheery hello to me, asking if I hadn't seen any more rabbits lately. Such notoriety one can live without. It's not just wild animals that can get you, it can be plants, too!

There are many poisonous plants which are irritating to humans and pets. In fact, more than seven hundred species of plants in the United States and Canada have caused illness at one time or another and the list is growing as research goes on. Some are rare plants; others you probably have in your garden. You might as well know and be warned. There are few true antidotes for poisoning by plants. A physician or veterinarian should be summoned immediately if a child or a pet is suspected of having eaten anything poisonous. Inducing vomiting might be the worse thing to do. I know you're not going to go around eating your wisteria vines, but small children are not always so sensible. Pretty red berries can be appealing to them.

Ready for a list of the culprits? You're in for a surprise. Some are such staunch standbys, popular since the year one, that it'll be a little like learning that your Aunt Mathilda has just run off with her hairdresser. Correction. It'll be worse.

Bulbs of hyacinth, daffodil and amaryllis. Leaves of poinsettia, Dumbcane, Christmas rose, caladium, philodendron. Mistletoe berries are for kissing under, not eating. Annual and perennial larkspur, monkshoods, lupines, iris, autumn crocus, lily-of-the-valley, snowdrops—their fleshy roots or bulbs are dangerous. Foxglove (leave it to the chemists to extract the digitalis from it) and poppy (opium is illegal so forget the idea). Bleeding heart contains stuff related to morphine. Would you believe that the sprouts on potatoes are toxic? The rhubarb *leaf* contains citric and oxalic acid which is highly toxic in large amounts.

197

The pods which follow the handsome flowers of the wisteria and goldenchain tree can cause severe digestive upsets when eaten. Three of the most beautiful shrubs to be found anywhere, mountain laurel, rhododendron and pieris, have lethal leaves. Did you know that the Delaware Indians used laurel for suicide? Well, now you can add that to your cocktail party chatter. Also poisonous is yew (the red berries are less powerful than the foliage, which causes instant death). Not as bad, but I wouldn't let the dog eat them, are boxwood and privet. You see what I mean? How commonplace can you get? You don't know what to trust, so the best thing to do is not to nibble plants, other than cultivated vegetables. I won't even go into plants found in the wild. But do stay away from those "wild carrots" growing along roadsides. They're not true wild carrots; they're poison hemlock, and remember what happened to Socrates.

I refrained from the obvious trio: Poison ivy, poison oak and poison sumac. You know all about them already. If you don't, get a knowledgeable neighbor to take you by the hand and point them out. If you're sensitive to one, you'll be sensitive to all three. And, you'll also be sensitive to Japanese lacquer. You didn't know? Add that to the cocktail chatter. Seems the poisonous element in these plants is very similar to that found in Japanese lacquer.

19

The Chic Trip Back to Nature

It's very "in" today to by-pass chemicals of all sorts and rely on natural control of pests and organically-derived fertilizers. People who have never so much as grown a pot of geraniums on the window sill of their city apartment are throwing around words like "composting" as if they had been born in a haystack.

Compost piles are springing up like mushrooms all around suburbia. The two-car family, which gave way to the private swimming pool-platform tennis court syndrome, has now progressed to the "compost pile" backyard, complete with the smug air of superiority that comes from knowing "what's the ecologically sound thing to do." This is all very well if you know what you're doing and why. Many books have been written about organic gardening, both for and against it—not against it in principle, but because of many half-truths and false claims that have been made in its name. I'm not about to get into the middle of this debate, but will only touch on the subject as it relates specifically to the gardener with very little time to spend on his plants.

Compost piles require time. You need two in order to have one always "cooked" and ready for use; otherwise, you have to scoop from underneath to get at the decomposed material. If you have the space and time, try it. The rich humus which you will get eventually (it takes time and a great deal of roughage to get even a small quantity of composted material) will be excellent to add to your flower beds each spring. A good chemical fertilizer scratched into the soil will do as well, however. Remember that the composted material—like a computer—is only as good as what you put into it. It will not contain nutrients that did not exist in the original roughage. Any mineral or other deficiencies must still be added. Similarly, any diseased material added to the compost pile will remain in it.

Mulching, which is given such emphasis in organic gardening, has, as you already know from the chapter on it, my total and full enthusiasm. I admit that my reasons are more for laziness' sake—but the end results are the same. Similarly, I have kept spraying, which is such a tedious, boring chore, to the barest minimum. There are some "natural controls" which help to deter insects. If you don't mind growing onions in your rose bed, they might prevent aphids. "Companion planting" is the term for putting plants together which will fight off one another's bugs. Strong-smelling, strong-tasting foliage of plants will send insects looking elsewhere for food. Considering the relatively small size of your garden, as a weekend no-time gardener, you might think twice before planting garlic in your only showcase flower bed. If you are really gone on the subject, however, do read *Companion Plants and How To Use Them*, by Helen Philbrick and Richard B. Gregg, $4.95, Devin-Adair Co.

20

What to Read—
What to Join—
Where to Write for Help—
Where to Buy Plants

I don't believe it. Here you started out reluctantly poking around the garden, your eyes fixed on the car in the driveway with its motor running and golf clubs in the back, cursing the lawn mower for going too slowly. That was you, remember? That gardening bit has really gotten under your skin, hasn't it? Welcome to the club. It can be fun, as you've found out, *if* you keep it under control and know what you're doing.

You can still learn a great deal more. If, after you've been gardening a few years, you find yourself liking it better and better, you'll also feel the need to go into it more deeply. This you can do easily. Winter is the ideal time to read books, pore through catalogs, attend lectures, make notes.

It's true that you learn mainly through doing, but reading as you go along is of tremendous importance. You needn't go all out and buy dozens of books. All you need is a good basic reference book, one or two volumes on specialized subjects which cover what you're presently growing (like perennials), and perhaps one book on something that you're not currently involved with but might wish to go into in greater depth (such as rock gardens). The list which follows is current as of this date, but prices may change. This does not mean that excellent books haven't been published before, but if these are out of print or hard to obtain, it would require a good deal of effort on the part of your dealer to get his hands on copies. Besides, the whole field of horticulture is constantly changing, due to intensive research and development of improved plant material.

If you get really hooked on a particular plant, you'll be happy to know that you have lots of fellow hobbyists. There is a plant society for each of the more popular breeds. Let's say you've discovered that you have fantastic talent for fuchsias. Thanks to your tender care and the right climate, you have baskets dripping with the lush plants, hanging from every tree on your property. You've turned into the "Sorcerer's apprentice." By joining the fuchsia society, you'll be able to read their publication, which will keep you up-to-the-minute on all the latest hybrid varieties, propagation, fertilization, etc. Members exchange cuttings and cozy "in" chatter.

What to Read

General Books:

America's Garden Book, James & Louise Bush-Brown, Scribner. $10.00
Taylor's Encyclopedia of Gardening, Norman Taylor, Houghton Mifflin. $12.95
Wyman's Gardening Encyclopedia, Donald Wyman, Macmillan. $17.50

Trees—Shrubs—Ground Covers—Vines:

Dwarf Conifers, H.J. Welch, Branford. $15.00
Evergreens, James U. Crockett, Time-Life. $6.95
Handbook of Hollies, Holly Society of America, Box 8445, Baltimore, Maryland 21234. $5.50
Rhododendrons and Azaleas, Clement Gray Bowers, Macmillan. $15.00
Shrubs and Vines for American Gardens, Donald Wyman, Macmillan. $10.95
The Complete Book of Ground Covers, Robert E. Atkinson, McKay. $7.95
The Guide To Garden Shrubs and Trees, Norman Taylor, Houghton Mifflin. $8.95
Trees For American Gardens, Donald Wyman, Macmillan. $14.95

Fruits—Vegetables—Herbs:

Dwarf Fruit Trees Indoors and Outdoors, Robert Atkinson, Van Nostrand and Reinhold. $7.95
Gardening with Herbs, Helen Morgenthau Fox, Sterling. $4.50. Also paperback, Dover. $2.50
Herbs for Every Garden, Gertrude B. Foster, Dutton. $4.95
The Green Thumb Book of Fruit and Vegetable Gardening, George Abraham, Prentice-Hall. $7.95

Annuals—Perennials—Bulbs:

Annuals, James U. Crockett, Time-Life. $6.95
Contemporary Perennials, Roderick W. Cumming, Macmillan. $6.95
Dahlias For Everyone, T.H.R. Lebar, St. Martin's. $3.95
Ferns to Know and Grow, F. Gordon Foster, Hawthorn. $7.95
Hardy Garden Bulbs, Gertrude S. Wister, Dutton. $5.95
Irises, Harry Randall, Taplinger. $8.95
Lilies, de Graaff & Hyams, Funk & Wagnalls. $6.95
The Chrysanthemum Book, Roderick W. Cumming, Van Nostrand. $7.95
Handbook of Wild Flower Cultivation, Kathryn S. Taylor and Stephen B. Hamblin, Macmillan. $7.95
The Joy of Geraniums, Helen Van Pelt Wilson, Barrows. $3.25 paper
The Peonies, John C. Wister, American Horticultural Society. $3.50

Regional and Specialized:

The Art of the Japanese Garden, Tatsuo & Kiyolo Ishimoto, Crown. $4.50

Bonsai for Americans, George F. Hull, Doubleday. $6.95

Bonsai, Trees and Shrubs, Lynn R. Perry, Ronald. $7.50

Container Gardening Outdoors, George Taloumis, Simon & Schuster. $7.95

Diseases and Pests of Ornamental Plants, P.P. Pirone, Ronald. $12.00

Flora of Alaska and Neighboring Territories, Eric Hulten, Stanford University Press. $35.00

The Flora of New England, Frank Conkling Seymour, Tuttle. $13.75

Gardening By the Sea, Daniel J. Foley, Chilton. $6.95

Gardening in the East, Stanley Schuler, Macmillan. $9.95

Gardening Under Glass, Jerome A. Eaton, Macmillan. $8.95

Greenhouse Gardening as a Hobby, James Underwood Crockett, Doubleday. $5.95

Hanging Gardens: Basket Plants Indoors and Out, Jack Kramer, Scribner's. $5.95, $2.95 paper

How to Prune Almost Everything, John Philip Baumgardt, Barrows. $6.95, $2.45 paper

The Japanese Art of Miniature Trees and Landscapes, Yoshimura & Halford, Tuttle. $7.25 paper

Plant Disease Handbook, Cynthia Westcott, Van Nostrand and Reinhold. $19.95

Rock Gardening, H. Lincoln Foster, Houghton Mifflin. $7.00

The Salty Thumb, Montauk Village Association, Box 457, Montauk, New York 11954. $3.25

Southwest Gardening, Doolittle & Tiedebohl, University of New Mexico Press. $6.50, $2.45 paper

Tropical Planting and Gardening for South Florida and West Indies, Nixon Smiley, University of Miami Press, paperback. $3.95

Water Gardening, Jack Kramer, Scribner's. $5.95, $2.95 paper

The World of the Japanese Garden, Lorraine Kuck, Walker-Weatherhill. $17.50

While the above list may appear to be on the long side, it is merely a sampling, although in my opinion (and that of others), it's representative of some of the "giants" in the horticultural field. Your local horticultural society or public library will have many more to offer you. Unless you are blessed with "total recall" or are willing to take down copious notes, do invest in buying the few books that appeal to you. You will be referring to them over and over again. These are, after all, reference books, and should be treated as such.

There are two other sources of excellent handbooks which I cannot recommend highly enough. One is the Brooklyn Botanic Garden (1000 Washington Avenue, Brooklyn, New York 11225), whose "Handbooks" on dozens of topics from "Summer Flowers For Continuing Bloom" to "Gardening In The Shade" are concise, authoritative and easy to collect. They range from $1.00 to $1.50 apiece and are worth lots more. Send for their list.

The other is the group of "Sunset Gardening Books" (Lane Book Company, Menlo Park, California 94025). They cover just about anything having to do with enjoying life in the great outdoors—as Californians can do so superbly! Plant material, rock gardens, patios, decks, fences, gates, walks and walls, garden pools and fountains and of course (!) swimming pools, among others, are all expertly described. They're $1.95; a few cost a bit more. Send for their list also. It's well worth it. The one on pruning is one of the most concise, easy to understand, intelligently illustrated guides on that subject that I have run across.

What To Join

Plant Societies

(Yearly dues range from $1 to $5, but are subject to change)

African Violet Society
    of America, Inc.
    Box 1326
    Knoxville, Tennessee 37901

American Camellia Society
    Box 212
    Fort Valley, Georgia 31030

American Begonia Society, Inc.
    1431 Coronado Terrace
    Los Angeles, California 90026

American Daffodil Society, Inc.
    89 Chichester Road
    New Canaan, Connecticut 06840

American Dahlia Society, Inc.
92-21 W. Delaware Drive
Mystic Islands, Tuckerton,
New Jersey 08087

American Delphinium Society
c/o Mr. Arthur Brooks
Van Wert, Ohio 45891

American Fern Society
Department of Botany
University of Tennessee
Knoxville, Tennessee 37916

American Fuchsia Society
738 22nd Avenue
San Francisco, California 94121

American Gloxinia and Gesneriad
Society, Inc.
Department AHS
Eastford, Connecticut 06242

American Hemerocallis Society
Box 586
Woodstock, Illinois 60098

American Hibiscus Society
Box 98
Eagle Lake, Florida 33839

The American Horticultural
Society, Inc.
910 N. Washington Street
Alexandria, Virginia 22314

American Iris Society
2315 Tower Grove Avenue
St. Louis, Missouri 63110

American Peony Society
107½ W. Main Street
Van Wert, Ohio 45891

American Primrose Society
14015 84th Avenue N.E.
Bothell, Washington 97140

American Rock Garden Society
90 Pierpont Road
Waterbury, Connecticut 06705

American Rose Society
4048 Roselea Place
Columbus, Ohio 43214

The Bromeliad Society
1811 Edgecliffe Drive
Los Angeles, California 90026

The Cactus and Succulent Society
of America, Inc.
Box 167
Reseda, California 91335

The Canadian Rose Society
38 Golf Club Road
Toronto, Ontario, Canada

The Herb Society of America
300 Massachusetts Avenue
Boston, Massachusetts 02115

Holly Society of America, Inc.
Box 8445
Baltimore, Maryland 21234

International Geranium Society
1413 Shoreline Drive
Santa Barbara, California 93105

National Chrysanthemum
Society, Inc.
8504 La Verne Drive
Adelphi, Maryland 20763

North American Gladiolus Council
234 South Street
South Elgin, Illinois 60177

North American Lily Society
North Ferrisburg, Vermont 05473

Where to Write for Help

State agricultural colleges and universities are good sources of free, sound, professional advice. They have the added advantage of knowing exactly what problems you face (such as type soil, rockbeds, winds, rainfall, etc.) because they are obviously familiar with *your* state. Local botanical gardens fall in the same category. Some state colleges maintain experimental and test gardens which are well worth a visit. They also publish bulletins and circulars, and the list is available upon request. A soil testing service is offered to residents of the state by some colleges. The Agricultural Extension Service, which usually has its headquarters at the state college, and the local County Agricultural Agent are the most available and extensive sources to call upon when you are baffled about a particular problem.

Offices of Agricultural Extension Service

ALABAMA–Auburn University, Auburn, 36830
ALASKA–University of Alaska, College, 99701
ARIZONA–University of Arizona, Tucson, 85721
ARKANSAS–University of Arkansas, Box 391, Little Rock, 72203
CALIFORNIA–Agricultural Extension Service, 2200 University Avenue, Berkeley, 94720
COLORADO–Colorado State University, Fort Collins, 80521
CONNECTICUT–University of Connecticut, Storrs, 06268
DELAWARE–University of Delaware, Newark, 19711
FLORIDA–University of Florida, Gainesville, 32601
GEORGIA–University of Georgia, Athens, 30601
HAWAII–College of Tropical Agriculture, University of Hawaii, Honolulu, 96822
IDAHO–University of Idaho, Moscow, 83843
ILLINOIS–University of Illinois, Urbana, 61801

INDIANA–Purdue University, LaFayette, 47907

IOWA–Iowa State College of Agriculture, Ames, 50010

KANSAS–Kansas State College of Agriculture, Manhattan, 66502

KENTUCKY–University of Kentucky, Lexington, 40506

LOUISIANA–Louisiana State University, University Station, Baton Rouge, 70803

MAINE–University of Maine, Orono, 04473

MARYLAND–University of Maryland, College Park, 20705

MASSACHUSETTS–University of Massachusetts, Amherst, 01002

MICHIGAN–Michigan State College of Agriculture, East Lansing, 48823

MINNESOTA–University of Minnesota, St. Paul, 55101

MISSISSIPPI–Mississippi State University, State College, 39762

MISSOURI–University of Missouri, Columbia, 65201

MONTANA–Montana State University, Bozeman, 59715

NEBRASKA–University of Nebraska, Lincoln, 68503

NEVADA–University of Nevada, Reno, 89507

NEW HAMPSHIRE–University of New Hampshire, Durham, 03824

NEW JERSEY–Rutgers University, New Brunswick, 08903

NEW MEXICO–New Mexico State University, Las Cruces, 88001

NEW YORK–Cornell University, Ithaca, 14850

NORTH CAROLINA–North Carolina State College of Agriculture, Raleigh, 27607

NORTH DAKOTA–North Dakota Agricultural College, State College Station, Fargo, 58102

OHIO–College of Agriculture, Ohio State University, Columbus, 43210

OKLAHOMA–Oklahoma State University, Stillwater, 74074

OREGON–Oregon State University, Corvallis, 97331

PENNSYLVANIA–Pennsylvania State University, University Park, 16802

PUERTO RICO–University of Puerto Rico, Mayagues Campus, Box H, Rio Piedras, 00928

RHODE ISLAND–University of Rhode Island, Kingston, 02881

SOUTH CAROLINA–Clemson University, Clemson, 29630

SOUTH DAKOTA–South Dakota State University, Brookings, 57000

TENNESSEE–University of Tennessee, Knoxville, 37901

TEXAS–Texas Agricultural College, College Station, 77843

UTAH–Utah State University, Logan, 84321

VERMONT–University of Vermont, Burlington, 05401

VIRGINIA–Virginia Polytechnic Institute, Blacksburg, 24061

WASHINGTON–Washington State University, Pullman, 99163

WEST VIRGINIA–West Virginia University, Morgantown, 26506

WISCONSIN–University of Wisconsin, Madison, 53813

WYOMING–University of Wyoming, Laramie, 82070

Where to Buy Plants

Mail Order Nurseries For General Plant Material:

George W. Park Seed Co., Inc., Greenwood, South Carolina 29646
Stern's Nurseries, Geneva, New York 14456
Wayside Gardens, Mentor, Ohio 44060
White Flower Farm, Litchfield, Connecticut 06759

Specialized Mail Order Nurseries:

American Perennial Gardens, 6975 Dover Street, Garden City, Michigan 48135 (Perennials)
Bunting's Nurseries, Inc., Selbyville, Delaware 19975 (Berries, fruits)
Caprilands Herb Farm, Silver Street, Coventry, Connecticut 06238 (Herbs)
Cook's Geranium Nursery, 712 North Grand, Lyons, Kansas 67554 (Geraniums)
Edelweiss Gardens, 54 Robbinsville-Allentown Road, Robbinsville, New Jersey 08691 (Begonias, ferns, cacti and succulents, bromeliads)
Henry Leuthardt Nurseries, Inc., East Moriches, New York 11940 (Dwarf fruit trees, berries)
Logee's Greenhouses, 55 North Street, Danielson, Connecticut 06239 (Begonias, geraniums, herbs, rare plants)
Manhattan Garden Supply, 305 North Sepulveda Blvd., Manhattan Beach, California 90266 (Geraniums)
Merry Gardens, Camden, Maine 04843 (Herbs, geraniums, begonias, ferns, vines, cacti and succulents, fuchsias)
New York State Fruit Testing Cooperative Association, Geneva, New York 14456 (Fruits, berries)
Oliver Nurseries, 1159 Bronson Road, Fairfield, Connecticut 06430 (Rhododendrons, azaleas, pines, rock garden evergreens)
Orinda Nursery, Bridgeville, Delaware 19933 (Camellias)
P. De Jager & Sons, Inc., South Hamilton, Massachusetts 01982 (Flower bulbs)
Putney Nursery, Inc., Putney, Vermont 05346 (Wildflowers, perennials, herbs)
Rayner Brothers, Inc., Salisbury, Maryland 21801 (Berries, fruits)

209

Road Runner Ranch, 2458 Catalina Avenue, Vista, California 92083 (Geraniums)

Ruth Hardy's Wildflower Nursery, Falls Village, Connecticut 06031 (Wildflowers)

S. Scherer & Sons, Waterside Road, Northport, New York 11768 (Water lilies and other aquatic plants)

Stark Bros., Louisiana, Missouri 63353 (Fruits)

Three Springs Fisheries, Lilypons, Maryland 21717 (Water lilies and other aquatic plants)

Vetterle Bros., P.O. Box 7, Capitola, California 95010 (Tuberous begonias)

Wilson Brothers, Roachdale, Indiana 46172 (Geraniums)

Special Note:

There is an excellent handbook put out by the Brooklyn Botanic Garden, called "1,200 Trees and Shrubs—Where to Buy Them."

Index